SUGERFAN
HOW POP CULTURE
BROKE MY HEART

"*Superfan* is a book you will want to simultaneously hug close to your chest and press insistently into others' hands. There is such honesty, intelligence, warmth, and vulnerability to these essays that, when you finally put them down, you'll feel breathless—a little sad it's over, but ultimately full, invigorated, as if you've just ended an evening of deep, intimate conversation with your best friend. It takes a rare talent to pull this feat off—and Jen Sookfong Lee is that talent. I love this book."

—**ALICIA ELLIOTT**, author of *A Mind Spread Out on the Ground*

"*Superfan* is about how deeply and, sometimes, disappointingly personal pop culture can be, even and especially for those of us for whom it's not made. As she explores her identity through the books, movies, and movie stars who accompanied her along the path of self-discovery, Jen Sookfong Lee has written a memoir that is gorgeous and ugly, generous and petty, wild and self-conscious. In the process, she defiantly claims the right to be the good girl, the bad girl, and all the transitions in between. A thoughtful and exhilarating and brave self-portrait of a woman demanding to be seen and who, at long last, is able to see herself." ·

—**ELAINE LUI**, author of *LaineyGossip* and
Listen to the Squawking Chicken

"*Superfan* vividly brings to life the joys and despair of obsessing over pop culture—both feeling seen by it and being deeply hurt by it. Lee's insights are devastating and tender, hilarious and profound. *Superfan*'s introspective meditations on familiar pop culture moments effortlessly turn them into relatable and heartbreaking vignettes. You know that thing when a scene in a movie destroys you, and you have to spend a week reassembling your life, but you don't know why? Lee has done the work to figure out why, and her writing about it is so vulnerable it might destroy you too."

—ELAMIN ABDELMAHMOUD, author of *Son of Elsewhere*

"*Superfan* is an extraordinary work of personal memoir and pop cultural criticism. Lee's exploration of pop culture's impact on her as a child of Chinese immigrants is brilliant, absurd, and heartbreaking, and she shares her stories with so much warmth and generosity that by the end you will feel like her best friend. Each chapter had me laughing out loud and underlining her provocative takes on subjects like 90s heartthrobs, Gwyneth Paltrow, and the Kardashians. Eye-opening and luminous and so much fun!"

—HEATHER O'NEILL, author of *When We Lost Our Heads*

"*Superfan* is a fresh reclamation of pop culture from an unexpected and exciting perspective. By juxtaposing her everyday life as an Asian woman with those of iconic TV characters and popstars, Jen Sookfong Lee spotlights how pop culture can be a mirror in which to both see and not see yourself, a gateway to somewhere else and a reminder of how stuck you are. It's this complexity that makes *Superfan* a fantastic read!"

—VIVEK SHRAYA, author of *People Change*

SUPERFAN

BOOKS BY JEN SOOKFONG LEE

NON-FICTION

Gentlemen of the Shade: My Own Private Idaho (2017)

Superfan: How Pop Culture Broke My Heart (2023)

FICTION

The End of East (2007)

The Better Mother (2011)

The Conjoined (2016)

POETRY

The Shadow List (2021)

ANTHOLOGIES

Whatever Gets You Through:
Twelve Survivors on Life after Sexual Assault
(co-edited with Stacey May Fowles, 2019)

Good Mom on Paper:
Writers on Creativity and Motherhood
(co-edited with Stacey May Fowles, 2022)

SUPERFAN

HOW POP CULTURE BROKE MY HEART

A MEMOIR

JEN SOOKFONG LEE

McCLELLAND & STEWART

McClelland & Stewart and colophon are registered trademarks
of Penguin Random House Canada Limited.

Library and Archives Canada Cataloguing in Publication data is
available upon request.

ISBN: 978-0-7710-2521-1
ebook ISBN: 978-0-7710-2522-8

Book design by Jennifer Griffiths
Cover photograph: Kyrani Kanavaros
Typeset in Heldane Text by M&S, Toronto
Printed in Canada

McClelland & Stewart,
a division of Penguin Random House Canada Limited,
a Penguin Random House Company
www.penguinrandomhouse.ca

1 2 3 4 5   27 26 25 24 23

Penguin
Random House
McCLELLAND & STEWART

In memory of
Soon Chung Park,
Hyun Jung Grant,
Suncha Kim,
Yong Ae Yue,
Xiaojie Tan,
and Daoyou Feng

ALL THE NAMES OF PRIVATE INDIVIDUALS
USED THROUGHOUT THIS BOOK,
WITH THE EXCEPTION OF MY OWN,
HAVE BEEN CHANGED.

CONTENTS

INTRODUCTION

I was born in 1976, into a noisy house in East Vancouver where there were never enough bathrooms, privacy, or salt and vinegar chips to go around. By the time I arrived, my four older sisters were between the ages of seven and seventeen, and I would, for many years, remain the smallest and most observant member of the household. I would often hide in corners and behind doors, where I could listen to the conversations swirling around me, and watch the teens and adults rush through their lives, slamming doors as they ran out to waiting cars or to catch the bus downtown. I patched together bits and pieces of gossip, old memories, and confessions, and wrote and rewrote the story of my family in my head, a circular reimagining that became a comfort as I grew older. During the years when it seemed our family was falling apart, picturing my grandfather stepping off a boat in Victoria in 1913 with his one bag and one Western-style suit was a balm, a reminder that he had launched himself into the great unknown for the children and grandchildren who had not yet been born. That kind of love felt supernatural, like a genetic prescience.

In our family, immigration from China was recent memory. My grandparents and parents spent much of their time outside the home using whatever tools they could to prove that they belonged in the country where they now lived. Popular culture—the soap operas, the fashion magazines, the celebrity gossip, and the hockey fandom— was how they found a way in, studying, learning, and parroting what the white people around them were consuming. For my grandfather, who paid the five-hundred-dollar head tax upon his arrival in Canada at age seventeen, it meant listening to CBC Radio all day long. For my father, who joined my grandfather in Vancouver after the Chinese Exclusion Act was lifted in 1947, it meant listening to Chuck Berry and dropping his accent as soon as he could. For my mother, who married a man she had only met in letters and photographs for the opportunity to leave Hong Kong, it meant learning to bake the perfect sponge cake. For my older sisters, it meant perming their hair and never missing an episode of *Dallas*. And for me, it meant taping New Kids on the Block songs off the radio and, later, sending love letters to Beck. These were all ways that we engaged with popular culture. These were the things we talked about at school and at the office, and whenever we walked into new situations where we were visibly different. Maybe we were missing privilege and whiteness, but we could watch what everyone else was watching and try to close the distance between *us* and *them*.

Pop culture also became the measure by which we judged ourselves, which was a relationship that was equal parts motivating and demoralizing. We might have worked hard to be as successful as Diane Keaton in *Baby Boom*, but we also had to contend with the growing realization that, while no one in the world was going to be as beautiful as Connie Sellecca on *Hotel* or Diane Lane in *The Outsiders*, my sisters and I were also never going to be as rich or as white. It didn't matter if my hair was permed in spiral curls, or if my sisters got their makeup done at the Lancôme counter, or if my father watched every single B.C. Lions football game; there was no way we could erase our faces—those smooth, olive-skinned, southern Chinese faces that betrayed our identities even if we would have rather stayed hidden.

♥

Beginning in my childhood, I started losing people. My mother, who was constantly fighting off anxiety and depression, would sometimes entirely disengage from our lives, retreating to her bedroom or sitting on the living room sofa, her silence suffocating the entire house. My father would get cancer and die, followed shortly by his own father. My sisters moved out one by one until, by the time I was nineteen, I was living in our old Vancouver Special alone with my mother. It's a special kind of torture to be the youngest child left behind, wandering through a house of empty bedrooms, picking through the eighties blouses and cheap drugstore perfumes your sisters didn't want to take with them.

Still, I couldn't help but be reminded every single day of the life my family once had when we were all together, when my father was alive, when my mother used to host mah-jong parties and laugh at naughty jokes with her friends. But as I grew older, the memories faded, receding into a murky dreamscape that I was pretty sure wasn't accurate. As I had done when I was younger, I began to stitch together what I knew to be real with connective tissue, small transitional fictions and a little magic realism to make my family whole again. Or at least to make our stories whole again.

I used pop culture in the same way, as a kind of glue to hold me together when I was hurtling through disaster. If I was lonely, I could listen to a Barenaked Ladies CD and imagine they were singing those lyrics of longing and disappointment to me, *for* me. If I was angry with my mother, I could reread *The Secret Garden*, where Mary's mother exists only in flashes of memory of her walking away from her only child, a beautiful lacy dress swirling around her ankles. In those moments, it didn't matter that I had never met singer-song-writer Steven Page, or that I wasn't a Victorian-era child exploring the English moors; it mattered only that one fragment of their stories fit into mine. I was so used to not fitting in at all, to being the extra daughter who was often forgotten, that jamming a piece of pop culture into an absence in my life, no matter how poorly matched, seemed fine. It seemed like the only, no, the *best* thing to do.

This is how I became a writer.

♥

I am not discriminating. All culture, high or low, is of equal impor-tance to me, whether I am sitting in a room at the Tate Modern lined with Mark Rothko paintings, or I'm intently watching an episode of *90 Day Fiancé*. There are always homilies to be borrowed, a conclu-sion to be made about the zeitgeist, a crush to be formed.

You remember the first time you fell in love with a celebrity, don't you? The first time you saw David Cassidy smile widely at the camera. The first time you heard a Florence + the Machine song soar through the speakers in your car. The first time you watched Sarah Jessica Parker walk down that Manhattan sidewalk in a white tutu.

Did your heart beat so strongly you feared it would burst through your chest? Did your vision narrow until all you saw was that person, tiny but seemingly real, on your screen? Did you cry when the lyrics became clear to you, a breaking open of meaning like storm clouds parting to reveal a blue sky you had forgotten? These revelations, these moments of parasocial love, can occur once in a lifetime or many times over. I am culturally polyamorous, a person who can maintain several celebrity relationships at once. The variety is essential; I take what I need from each to fill every gap in my real life.

This book is like a mixtape, a compilation of my most loved— and a couple of my most hated—cultural moments and the people who inspired them. Sometimes they comforted me. Sometimes they enraged me. Sometimes they threw my own failings, longings, and aspirations into stark relief. Sometimes they showed me solutions, potential problems, other ways of being. But they were my constant companions—there on lonely nights or quiet mornings, when I was so anxious I couldn't focus on anything but TMZ and the outlandish outfits at the Met Gala, after my marriage died and the bed I slept in felt impossibly vast.

Once upon a time, I might have thought that my love of pop culture was a passing phase, the sort of thing many sad teens use to distract themselves from the realities of their lives. But now, in my forties, I know that this is a forever relationship, one that has outlasted partners, friends, even dogs. It's fitting, isn't it, to write a tribute to the longest commitment of my life, one that has carried me from childhood to this very moment? Tonight, I will watch a music awards show and be mesmerized by Mary J. Blige's crystal-encrusted gown; the panning shots of the chaotic crowd and bright stage lights will feel like coming home to a family who both sees you and enrages you, who cares for you while borrowing your belt without asking, who intuitively knows what you need and sometimes withholds it. A messy, performative, gossipy family whose peripatetic heartbeat is comprised of scandals and product placements, relentless choruses and binge-watches. A family that carries you along with its irresistible momentum even when you are the one thing that is not like the others, even when you know, deep down, you don't belong. It doesn't matter anyway. I have cobbled together my own identities and memberships from the cultural storm for as long as I can remember. It's the only perfection I know.

THE
ORPHAN

In 1984, the year I turned eight years old, my father was diagnosed with nasopharyngeal cancer.

Before he moved to Canada at age thirteen, he had lived with his mother and three older sisters in a two-room house in one of the many small towns in China's Pearl River Delta, the name of which, translated into English, is Lone Tree Village. There, his neighbourhood of winding alleys and stone houses was built around central communal spaces: the well, the pig pen, the fire pit, and, most famously, the giant tree in the main square with its drooping, heavily canopied branches. He told me that their home's main source of heat was a coal-burning stove that, after generations of use, had coated the walls with a thick black layer of sticky dust. My father's illness, a particularly difficult cancer to treat, was one that was seen in many men of his generation who spent their childhoods in heavily polluted southern China, where foods preserved in salt were linked to a higher risk of health problems.

When he coughed at night, it was constant. If he slept, or if my mother managed to sleep as she lay beside him, I still don't know.

Not coincidentally, 1984 was also the year I read *Anne of Green Gables* for the first time.

Like most of my books at the time, this one came from the shelves in the dining room, where my four older sisters would leave the books they had finished. The Norton anthologies. *Scruples* by Judith Krantz. *Surfacing* by Margaret Atwood. Throughout my childhood, I owned very little that was mine alone; everything, from the frames of my glasses to my banana-seat bicycle, had been used by my sisters before me. I was accustomed to reading, and mostly abandoning, their books. Some were too sexy. Most were from their university English courses. But this boxed set containing the first three books in Lucy Maud Montgomery's Anne series, with its illustration of a sad-faced thin little girl, seemed meant for me. I was a thin little girl who was continually left alone, who worried about cancer and chemotherapy, and whose face in the mirror was almost always sad. Maybe this book could be mine.

♥

Scrappy, red-headed Anne Shirley, along with hockey players and maple syrup, may very well be Canada's most famous export. Tourists flock to Cavendish, P.E.I., Lucy Maud Montgomery's hometown and the inspiration for the fictional Avonlea. *Anne of Green Gables—The Musical* has been in production since 1965 in Canada and has toured to Tokyo and London. Screen adaptations crop up every generation, each emblematic of its era, with the most recent, *Anne with an E*, attempting to address issues of racism and colonialism. But each version tells the same story of Anne's abandonment, adoption, and propensity for mishaps, both domestic and social.

By the time I started reading the novels, Anne had become a

lucrative industry, in the same way that the Harry Potter series by J.K. Rowling would go on to dominate the entertainment world in the 2000s, extending far beyond the books themselves to spawn films, stage plays, even a theme park in Japan. Both Anne and Harry are orphans dealing with grief and loss and a world that seems to value them less than it does children with two living, affectionate parents. People love underdogs, and young readers, with their sensitive minds and developing emotional intelligence, often love to be immersed in the lives of fictional children who have suffered the biggest of losses: the deaths of their parents. Think of Mary in *The Secret Garden*, Oliver in *Oliver Twist*, Mowgli in *The Jungle Book*. It's a kind of grim reassurance. If these orphans could go on to accomplish great things, experience love, and build their own nurturing families, then maybe all children have the chance to do the same. Or, at least, that's what I believed.

My older sisters, tasked with the job of keeping me distracted while my father underwent surgery, radiation therapy, and chemotherapy, bought me the rest of the Anne series in small paperbacks that cost $3.50 each. That winter, I read them all, then I read them again, curled up on my bunk bed, my desk lamp twisted backward during stormy afternoons after school. My mother was rarely home from the hospital before five, when she cooked dinner in a fury before leaving the dishes for my sister Penny who was fifteen and had a Billy Idol–esque spiky haircut and me to clean, both of us deemed too young to watch our father vomit and cry into the evening. While we ate—my mother at the head of the table, my sisters on the sides, and my paternal grandfather tucked into the small space by the window—the phone would ring. It was my oldest sister, Wendy, who had moved to Toronto with her husband to complete her M.B.A., calling for a daily update on my father's health. At six-thirty, my mother returned to the hospital with Daisy and Jackie—my two middle sisters, both in their twenties but still living at home—until visiting hours were over. When their car pulled back into the driveway, I was often already asleep, books splayed open on the floor beside me, spines cracked at the passages I had read over and over.

I have my old copy of *Anne of Green Gables* even now, and it always falls open to page 203, when Anne meets her mentor and teacher, Miss Stacy, who sees Anne's passions as an asset and encourages her to perform and write. "We have to write compositions on our field afternoons and I write the best ones," Anne tells Matthew and Marilla, the middle-aged brother and sister who have adopted her. I never spoke of my own school accomplishments at home: the short story that won the school contest, the spelling bee during which I came in second behind the only teacher who also competed, that one time I performed more sit-ups in a row than anyone else. These were small successes that made me feel valued for a day, maybe two, before I remembered that there were darker, more important things to worry about.

Back then, my mother didn't say much, caught as she was in a tornado of doing, caring, and surviving. She had come to Canada to be a bride in a marriage that was not entirely arranged but not entirely of her own choosing either. In 1958, the year she arrived, people in Hong Kong were already looking ahead to the day in 1997 when the colony would cease to be part of the Commonwealth and be returned to China's governance. I grew up hearing stories of women like my mother who looked for potential husbands to get them far away from the looming threat of Communist China. My father, a Canadian citizen whose family was firmly established in Vancouver but whose origins were in a small Chinese village close to where my mother's extended family lived, seemed like a wise choice. He was handsome, employed, and wrote charming letters after their two mothers had made introductions via photographs sent in white-and-blue airmail envelopes. That was enough for my mother to believe she was in love, board a steamer for the very first time, and move to Vancouver to live in a tall Victorian house in Mount Pleasant with her new husband and his parents.

My mother married and had five daughters and never worked in any job for more than a year. Her opportunities for learning English were limited, and by the time I was born, my sisters were old enough to earn their own spending money, and my father's salary as an accountant negated the need for my mother to work outside the home. Her English fluency diminished, and she grew uncomfortable speaking it at all. When I was six, I remember my father and I convinced my mother to enrol in an English-conversation class. At the time, she had registered me for Chinese school, which I hated, on Tuesday and Thursday afternoons. The teachers taught us by rote, repeating sentences in Cantonese over and over again, their rulers banging out a relentless rhythm on the chalkboard.

"If I have to go to Chinese school," I declared, "then you have to go to English school."

My father laughed and said, "Jenny has a point." Later that week, he pulled out a catalogue of evening courses and circled the English-language class that was running at the high school three blocks away.

As he dialled the number to register my mother, he nodded and said, "So convenient. We should have thought of this years ago."

I can still picture my mother sitting at the kitchen table with a cup of tea, staring into the middle distance, her face folding in on itself as if she were about to cry.

She lasted two classes before dropping out. "The teacher hates me." She shrugged. We never spoke of it again.

My father became the husband who filed the taxes, completed the forms, and met with the teachers, while my mother remained where she felt safe: in our home and in the shops of Vancouver's Chinatown.

Years later, my mother told me that while my father was fighting his cancer, she spent long nights worried about what would become of her in a country whose languages she did not speak and whose systems were unintelligible to her. She was a woman who had married at nineteen, who had never lived alone, who had been coddled by her mother because she was the pretty daughter with the pretty singing voice. She had been given few tools for her eventual life as a stay-at-home mother, managing the lives of five daughters whose future plans were focused on universities and executive careers. My sisters and I, speaking in fast-paced, slang-filled English, left her out of our conversations about school or work or the latest episode of *Knots Landing*. When we watched television, she stayed in her bedroom, listening to Canto-pop cassettes her sisters-in-law sent her from Hong Kong. Back then, I noticed the fear creep across her face whenever a stranger spoke to her in English—a bus driver, a sales lady at Woodward's, the mailman. Rather than answer, she pushed me in front of her so I could translate both the language and the social codes. When my father stayed overnight at the hospital, I could hear my mother weeping. I heard her. As clearly as I heard my father's rattling cough when he was home.

♥

In *Anne of the Island*, the third book in the series, Anne is on a break from her studies at Redmond College and visits her birth home in Bolingbroke, where her parents, a young couple named Walter and Bertha, had been schoolteachers. It's in this "shabby yellow house in an out-of-the-way street" where a woman gives her a bundle of letters—found in the closet upstairs and tied with a faded ribbon—that Walter and Bertha had written to each other over the course of their relationship. Through these letters, Anne discovers that her parents were very much in love, that she was a deeply anticipated baby, and that their family was, in the brief time they were all together, as flawless as a family could be, good people who lived good lives. They were well-liked in their community. They had plans for the future. And, most importantly, they had *wanted* Anne.

Although this scene in *Anne of the Island* is brief, it's hard not to feel a pang of pity for Marilla, who is first described in *Anne of Green Gables* as "a woman of narrow experience and rigid conscience." She is certainly not beautiful or young or in love, and Anne never imagines a romantic narrative about her past, as she does about Bertha. Marilla believes in hard work, in a decorous life, in plain Protestant virtue. She denies Anne a puffed-sleeve dress, until Matthew goes ahead and buys one for her himself. In the face of Marilla's rigidity and unadorned life, Anne often turns to other women—pretty, younger women, like Miss Stacy and Mrs. Allan—for advice.

Growing up, I had many substitute mothers, women I turned to for the kind of comfort and understanding that my mother, terrified of losing her husband and the life he had built for her, was unable to provide. During the years my father was sick, there was Donna from church, who listened to my worries, and my friend Mia's mother, Brigitte, who let us doodle on a designated living room wall. There was Mrs. Madison from school, who called me her "talented little writer." When my mother used up all her energy in caring for my father, managing our family, and, later, fighting a deep depression that lasted my entire adolescence, it was these women who hugged me, told funny stories, and said I was doing okay, even if it was abundantly clear that I was not. It was Donna who cleaned the wounds on my shins, where I was scratching the skin raw, my insides wound so tight with anxiety that I wanted to break open the surface of my body with my fingernails to release the tension. I saw myself in the orphan Anne. And I saw other, more perfect, mothers everywhere.

In the end, however, Marilla becomes the mother that Anne has always needed, a firm ballast whenever Anne finds herself lost in a tumble of emotions. And, in the process, Anne softens Marilla's angles so that she permits laughter, sadness, and empathy to escape her thorny exterior. In the books, motherhood—real, working motherhood—isn't pretty. While Bertha might have been beautiful and expressive, she isn't the one who gives Anne stability or an education or a moral centre. It's Marilla, the broken-hearted spinster who lives with her bachelor brother, who does that. It's Marilla who encourages Anne to attend university at a time when most young women didn't. It's Marilla who travels to care for Anne during the births of her children.

Before we know what she is capable of giving Anne, Marilla was my mother in novel form: disapproving, defined by rules, unable to express the roil of emotions under her skin. She had never displayed much maternal empathy, not even when my father was healthy. When my mother was at home, the only words she spoke were orders about meal prep or laundry, or she would sometimes rage about small mistakes: a ball of hair in the shower drain, spilled juice in the fridge, a hole in the seat of my pants from climbing a tree. I don't remember her asking us how we were doing, what school was like, if we were seeing our friends.

What I remember most from the years when my father was healthy was how my mother cooked a multicourse lunch every Sunday. The menu betrayed our Chinese Canadian tastes, with dishes that flirted with Chinese authenticity but were hybrids of my parents' origins and their current lives. There was chow mein, congee with fish and roasted peanuts, sweet and sour pork, and a bowl of warmed-up peas, corn, and carrots from a frozen Green Giant bag. Any of our friends could be invited to join us, from my sisters' boyfriends and my best friend Ronni to the girl my sister Wendy tutored in math. Everyone was welcome and my mother greeted each guest with a smile and mug of black tea. Conversation was shouted across our long kitchen table, with chopsticks clattering in bowls and my father's chuckle like a bassline, subtextual but omnipresent. Everyone complimented my mother's cooking, and she beamed, as if this was what she had always wanted.

But when it came time to clean up, my mother's mood would shift dramatically. With our company out of earshot in the basement family room, she commanded us to clear, rinse, wash, and dry, and expected silence from us in return. Leftovers had to be transferred to the ceramic containers, not the plastic ones, which were reserved for school and work lunches. We could not dirty a clean spoon to pack the food away. Instead, we had to find a utensil that had already been used during lunch. There was one tea towel for drying dishes and another for wiping down counters and they could not be mixed up. Not one drop of water could be left on a dish. Not one. Any misstep could unleash a storm of insults and accusations, all with my mother at the centre, a self-identified victim.

Ungrateful, useless daughters.

Why do you think you're so smart? You're stupid, anyone can see.

You're all just waiting for me to die.

Once in a while, she was happy—when she talked on the phone with her brother in Toronto, or when my father would bring home her favourite coconut cream bun—in fleeting moments that would later require effort for me to remember. And yet, in the before, there had at least been something.

But after my father's diagnosis, her moods grew darker. She was grieving and scared, unable to break out of her anxiety to see that the lives of her daughters were continuing, despite their father's cancer. Eight years old, confused and worried, I needed the comfort of knowing that not all mothers were perfect, that it was okay if they weren't all tolerant and pretty and interested in the small lives of their children. It was okay if they didn't speak English. If they collapsed in bed without saying one word to their youngest daughter, pulled the covers over their head, and cried themselves to sleep. Because maybe, eventually, they might say the loving words their children needed to hear.

Near the end of *Anne of Green Gables*, Marilla, changed by years of parenting, opens up to Anne. "You blessed girl!" she says after Anne decides to stay home and delay her university education. "I feel as if you'd given me new life." In a few years, I hoped, my own mother might say something just like that.

♥

One November afternoon two years later, my mother noticed me reading on the couch, angled so the dim light from the table lamp illuminated my copy of *Anne of the Island*, the Anne book I had reread the most, chiefly because of her romantic interests. (This was a fantasy that my nascent boy-crazy brain was just beginning to find exciting.)

From the kitchen, my mother glared at me and yelled, "How long have you been reading that?"

I looked up in surprise. It had been a very long time since my mother had noticed anything I did, especially something as commonplace and innocuous as reading. I struggled to remember when I'd picked up the book, but I couldn't. It had likely been at least two hours, ever since I had come home from school. "I don't know," I mumbled.

"Stop reading and help me cook dinner." My mother pointed her spatula in my direction. "Now."

"No," I said. I felt no obligation to help her. After all, she had barely uttered my name in months. I calmly continued to read my book.

Without saying another word, my mother, furious and almost certainly emotionally and physically exhausted, marched into the living room and pulled the book out of my hands. I followed her as she walked into my bedroom and swept all of my Anne books off their designated shelf and into her apron.

"Stay here until I come back," she barked as she carried the books away. I did as I was told. From the doorway, I could hear her moving objects in the kitchen, muttering as she dragged a chair across the linoleum floor. Waiting, I wondered if my father had grown sicker, if the treatments were not working as they should, if maybe this had flipped a rage switch in my mother's brain. I could have asked, but I knew better.

When she returned, she said, "I hid them. You're not getting them back until you help me cook dinner."

In the kitchen, she stood at the stove, a blazing hot wok in front of her. Instead of standing beside her so I could watch and therefore anticipate what ingredient she needed next (something I had watched my sisters try to do, with mixed success, all of my life), I sat down on the floor with my back against the refrigerator. I had no plan; I only knew that I was angry. If I couldn't have what I wanted, my mother wouldn't either. When she turned around to open the fridge door, I was right there to block her.

"What are you doing? Get up. I need to get to the fridge."

"No. I'm not moving."

"I don't understand."

"I'm not moving until you give me back my books."

What my mother likely hadn't considered was that my books, and my Anne books in particular, were the only constants in my life. My oldest sisters were always busy trying to manage my father's insurance and health benefits. My sister Penny was a teenager now, spending most of her free time in the weights room at the high school, where building muscle mass gave her a way to control at least one thing when everything else was uncontrollable. My grandfather had fallen into a quiet depression, hiding in his room off the hallway as his only son grew sicker and sicker. There was very little time for anyone in our household to pay attention to me. I walked to and from school alone. I completed my homework alone. I was a talkative, restlessly social child, who chatted nonstop at school. (I remember my report card that year said, "It's a challenge for Jennifer to understand that sometimes her input isn't appropriate.") As soon as I entered our house, the silence enveloped me, and I hated it.

Like me, Anne Shirley was a talker, a child who craved affection and human connection, even from the adults who would never love her. Before she arrives in Avonlea to live with Marilla and Matthew, she creates imaginary playmates at the orphanage and the one family home where she was treated more as a nanny than an adopted child. In Avonlea, she finds her true family and is loved and celebrated for the sensitive, creative, and passionate little girl she is, not the decorous, quiet little girl Marilla might have once wished for.

Near the end of *Anne of Green Gables*, Matthew says, "Well now, I'd rather have you than a dozen boys, Anne. Just mind you that— rather than a dozen boys. Well now, I guess it wasn't a boy that took the Avery scholarship, was it? It was a girl—my girl—my girl that I'm proud of." In my own small, dark place, worried that my father would never get better, that I had ruined my parents' last chance to have a son by being the fifth and youngest girl, this affirmation was what I needed, even though it wasn't about me. This comfort was what I turned to when there was no one to notice what I had eaten for my after-school snack or to read my new short story. In that kitchen, while the winter rain rattled the steamed-up windows, the injustice of having this small comfort stolen from me lit an intense rage.

I remember my mother stood in front of me. I knew she was thinking of pushing me aside, something that would be hard for her to do if I was determined to hold my ground. At ten years old, I was already my mother's height. I also knew my father was, at that very moment, lying in a hospital bed, a thin curtain separating him from another man who was succumbing to a brain tumour and who cried for his sons long into the night. My mother spent most of her waking hours brewing medicinal soups and bringing them to my father in a green Thermos, hoping something might help. She brushed his teeth, trimmed his nails, held him upright when he sat on the toilet.

This was not the moment to fight.

She pulled a chair from the table, climbed on the seat, and opened a high cupboard, where my books were piled behind a stack of rice bowls. She dropped them, one by one, onto the floor. *Anne of Green Gables. Anne of Avonlea. Anne of the Island. Anne of Windy Poplars. Anne's House of Dreams. Anne of Ingleside.* "There," she said quietly. "You win."

I picked them up and walked directly back to my room. For the first time in months, I felt happy, the anger ebbing away into satisfaction. It's only now that I see how sad and small a victory this was.

♥

In later books, Anne learns to control her passions, to muffle her temper, to wear fashionable clothes, in a concerted effort to calm her intensity. When I was eight, this seemed like success to me, or at least a success that I understood. That year, I began having panic attacks at school, for reasons that were seemingly unrelated to my father's illness. One morning, I arrived at my classroom after the bell had rung. I panicked in the cloakroom, hyperventilating behind a row of coats, crying and thrashing so hard that my teacher had to hold me to keep me from accidentally punching the walls. Days later, that same teacher was reading aloud stories my class had written when the bell rang before she got to mine. I burst into tears and didn't stop sobbing until she pulled me to her in a tight hug, once again holding me so I couldn't hurt myself as my body tried to kick out its frustrations. She wrote a letter to my parents: "We are working with Jennifer to help her learn that not every small mistake is a catastrophe."

I was often angry, exploding at friends for small slights, raging during a group project about the government of Japan because a classmate's punctuation was wrong. Other times, I was paralyzed with fear, sitting alone at my desk after the recess bell had rung, afraid none of the other children would acknowledge me on the playground. After that, on the recommendation of the principal, I visited our school counsellor every week in a corner of the library, where I was allowed to pick an item from a table of toys while she asked gentle questions about what scared me and what I liked about myself. "I'm good at school," I said. I remember that she paused with a Jenga block in her hand. "Is that what you like about yourself, or is that what everyone else likes about you?"

What I wanted most was to no longer worry, to no longer panic that one tiny misstep would unleash a chain of disastrous events, leading, as all of the dystopian visions in my panic attacks led, to my family being torn apart. Sometimes I feared an unexpected death: a city bus hurtling toward us, hitting only Penny and me while leaving everyone else screaming in terror. Sometimes I feared that my sisters would be kidnapped one by one until only I was left. Sometimes I imagined a man in a black top hat slowly walking up the sidewalk toward our house. What he would do when he arrived was amorphous, a shapeless cloud of evil. But I knew he would destroy everything and we would be separated, never to find each other again.

I never let myself wonder what would happen after my father died. Maybe all of these monstrous possibilities. Maybe something else entirely that I could not, or would not, imagine.

With my brain in a spiral, I turned to Anne. Instead of swirling in anxiety, I was in Avonlea, standing at the shore of the Lake of Shining Waters.

At eighteen, Anne attends university and dreams of becoming an author; in the end, she sets aside her ambitions to marry Gilbert Blythe and raise six children. Anne channels her creative energy into her family. She no longer experiences her rage or any true passions outside of domestic life. She gardens. She mothers. She tells stories to her children.

This calmness—the possibility of becoming an adult without dark thoughts, with a beautiful home and the kind of family that the world recognizes as valuable and worthy of praise—was a fantasy I buried myself in every single day. One day, I wouldn't care if anyone read my stories or not. One day, I might marry a doctor like Gilbert, who would know what to do if anyone fell sick. One day, I could shape a noisy, affectionate, tightly bonded family of my own. And there would be nothing left to fear.

♥

In 1988, the year I turned twelve, my father died.

I answered the phone when our family doctor called and asked to speak to my mother. It was a Saturday morning in September, and I was getting ready for Chinese school, which I was still attending, six years after my mother had dropped out of her English classes. I remember the doctor called my mother weekly, explaining to her the details of my father's treatments in Cantonese, which the oncologist at the hospital didn't speak. He didn't usually phone on Saturdays, but I didn't consider what a weekend call might mean, so I silently passed the phone to my mother as she packed another day's worth of food for my father, which, by then, he rarely ate. If he tried, he would usually throw it back up before tearfully apologizing. "I'm sorry," he would whisper. "It's such a waste."

I remember my mother snatching at the phone, in a hurry to get the day started. "Hello," she snapped, a tightness in her face. But then as she listened with the receiver pressed against her ear, her features loosened, as if her face was drooping, as if her muscles could no longer hold up to the strain. I remember her screaming for my sister Jackie before she dropped the phone and collapsed in a heap on the kitchen floor.

I have replayed that moment many times in my life, and the hour we spent with my father's body in the palliative care ward at Mount Saint Joseph Hospital in East Vancouver. It was a small room, with a tiny closet that fit one change of clothes and a coat. There was a television mounted in a corner near the ceiling. The curtains were open, and it was sunny. In the bed, my father was lying partially upright, as he had been doing lately to lessen the constant ache in his throat. His skin was grey and yellow at the same time, an impossibility in life and an unmistakable sign of death. His mouth was open, as if he had died while calling out in pain, as if he had been calling out for us—his five daughters, his wife, anyone who knew him from before. When he was a teenaged boy walking the Stanley Park seawall with his father. When he was a handsome young accountant in a Glen plaid suit with the pretty wife who sang Doris Day songs in her high voice. When he was a father teaching his girls to play badminton and to never, ever rely on a man for their livelihoods.

My mother held his face in her hands and wailed, "What were you trying to tell me?"

I turned away then and began to empty the contents of his closet into a plastic Safeway bag I had found on a shelf. A nurse gently took the bag away from me and whispered, "Don't worry about that." But I did worry. Because worrying was what I had always done best.

♥

Near the end of *Anne of Green Gables*, Matthew dies after reading about the collapse of the bank where he had invested the family's savings. This chapter—in which Anne is unable to cry, and she and Marilla have to reorganize their lives without Matthew and without money—was the one I read over and over, weeping at his death and the aftermath. Even as a teenaged girl, I knew that when I cried reading about Matthew, I was really crying for my father.

In the years that followed, my periods of anxiety would spike and wane. At its worst, when my marriage was ending, I experienced panic attacks up to seven times a week. The promise of a peaceful, contented life, in a big house, surrounded by children, never materialized for me, even when I lived in a big house and was a stay-at-home mother to my son. When it came time for my ex-husband and me to divide our library, I found all of my Lucy Maud Montgomery books in a box in the basement, and at the age of thirty-eight, I read them yet again. The separation had left me shell-shocked, sleepless, and worried about how my son and I would survive, but I slipped into Anne's story as easily as I ever had.

The last Anne book, *Rilla of Ingleside*, chronicles World War One, with all three of Anne's sons enlisting as soldiers. Jem and Shirley return, but Walter dies in battle. One of his poems, about the cost of war and reminiscent of "In Flanders Fields," is read around the English-speaking world, and he becomes, in death, a famous writer. Rilla, Anne's youngest daughter, fears she has also lost her sweetheart to war after communication between them falls silent. In the end, he comes back for her, a white scar running down his face, and the promise of love is hers again. An older, traumatized love but love nonetheless.

Newly separated and raw, I read this and cried. I realized then that this happy ending of Anne's was no happy ending at all. War had scarred or taken each of her children. Her red hair, which once symbolized her unruly emotions, turned white. Her happiness as a wife and mother, it seems, was temporary, and no defence against death or war.

Anxiety, for me anyway, is often about searching for the magical *one thing* I could do to make everything better, even when I know that there is no solution, no list I could make or email I could write to change the outcome. The idea that Anne could only earn her peaceful happiness for so long, by suppressing her anger and ambitions and wandering brain, was a comfort far different from the comfort I sought as a child. There was nothing that even she, the irrepressible Anne, could do to stop the war from coming, in the same way there was nothing I could have done to prevent my father from dying, and nothing I could do now to change the decisions I'd made during the last years of my marriage. Perhaps acceptance is the antidote to our fear of disaster.

♥

Anne lost her birth parents and, later, a child. She was an orphan who was given a loving home with the Cuthberts, as well as a community who accepted her shortcomings and celebrated her successes. Later, she created a family of her own, with a loving husband and children who adored her. And then, in the end, she loses her son, her life bookended by mirrored traumas. Her happiness rises and then falls again. Like mine. Like yours. Like everyone's.

THE
ARTIST

My childhood, in memory, is divided in two. There was the time before my father was diagnosed with cancer, and there was the time after. I was eight when he began coughing up blood and going to bed right after dinner. The before, when my father was still going to work every day, when he could run up the big hill on Kaslo Street, is foggy. I have only a handful of memories from that time that I tell to my son, over and over again, hoping that, in the telling, they stay bright and sharp and real.

1982

I am six years old and my father is working as an accountant at a company that wholesales tires, in an office off the Lougheed Highway in Coquitlam, a half-hour drive on a good day from our home in East Vancouver. In bad weather, it could take my father up to an hour to return home. Tonight, there is a snowstorm. Outside, the flakes are fat and heavy, falling straight down on the lawn and sidewalk to form perfect, smooth layers. My bedroom faces the street, and I watch the garden disappear and the light of the street lamps reflect like diamonds on the surface of the snow. It's quiet, preternaturally bright.

It's five o'clock, then six o'clock, then seven. My mother paces from the kitchen to the living room, stopping to peer out every window on her path, cracking the oven to check that my father's dinner is still warm.

My father is the kind of man who attends all our parent-teacher conferences and does the tax returns for his friends. My father is never late.

"The hill," she says, as she walks down the hallway once more. "He might not make it up the hill." Our house stands at the top of one of the many hills in East Vancouver, sloping south toward Still Creek, and also sloping north toward the industrial waterfront that borders the inlet. In order to get home, there is no avoiding the drive upward.

When I hear the sound of the exterior garage door opening, I run down the stairs, shouting, "Dad's home! Dad's home!" My mother runs with me and wrenches open the interior garage door in the hallway. The station wagon is covered in snow, but there is my father, emerging from the driver's side in his grey coat and wool hat. My mother hugs him and starts to cry, her face in his collar.

"One day," he says, looking at me, "I will retire and buy a pottery wheel and never have to drive in the snow again." I imagine my father, hands covered in wet clay, contentedly perfecting the roundness of vases and mugs and bowls, while I watch, sitting with an open book in the corner. We didn't know then that this would never happen.

♥

I do not know how much of this memory is true and how much of it is invented. I can still hear the shuffle of my father's slippers up the stairs as I lead him to his dinner, the rumble of his laughter as he hangs his sopping-wet coat to dry beside the heater. But they could be ghost sounds, from a time that never existed at all.

As a writer, making narrative out of the mess of life is nothing new for me. My psychologist once said, "This is what you do to feel in control when things are uncontrollable." I create stories. I tumble feelings into lines that can be moved, cut, and revised to include subtext and a dramatic arc. There is a pretend order that does not exist anywhere else.

I have lived most of my life without my father. It's hard to know if my memories of him are accurate or if they have accumulated so much storytelling, so much fictive magic, that the man I remember is no different than a character in one of my novels: an amalgam of people I have known, of people I wished I could be, of celebrities I think I know.

My relationship with his memory, then, is no different than my relationship with the famous people I have loved most: Keanu Reeves, Emma Thompson, Gord Downie, Kate Atkinson. With each of them, I saw someone to fall in love with, to emulate, to be my companion in sadness and also laughter. I knew them because of their fame, but my adoration came from my relationship with their work. Keanu grinned at the camera, but he was really grinning for me. Emma loved Jane Austen as much as I did. Gord sang me to sleep. And Kate wrote books about trauma and death that were also deeply funny, as I wished I could.

Perhaps this explains my intimacy with fandom, with my need to feel connected to people I have never met. After all, I never really knew my father. He lived for forty years before I was born and died before I could know him as anything more than a parent. He had thoughts that were never spoken out loud. He kept secrets. Sometimes, I imagine his past and inner life. Sometimes, I fall in love with a famous person and imagine what our life together could look like. Are these two daydreams really so different? It's the same act of filling gaps in knowledge and love with whatever I can, with words and fantasy and narrative. Because, for me, narrative has always been easy.

In the end, all I am left with are relationships made of nothing. There is no dad to call when my car breaks down, no Keanu to spoon when the nights are long and cold. Just me, and layers of fantasy that can never add up to a real person.

1985

It's after dinner and my dad is in a good mood. He turns on the radio in the kitchen and holds out his hands to me. "Let's dance, Jenny," he says, before launching into his version of the twist—slow and low to the ground, as if he is a very lazy drill bit inching closer and closer to its destination. When a ballad comes on, he picks me up and places my feet on his, and we do the box step in wide circles across the brown linoleum. Our house is usually full and noisy, with my sisters running in and out, hair in curlers or makeup half done, my grandfather hiding behind the newspaper in any corner he can find, the phone ringing every few minutes. And yet I don't hear or see anyone else in the kitchen. Just my dad and me, calmly dancing in ever-widening circles, a ballad by Billy Ocean or Wham! rolling through the air.

♥

"In painting, you have unlimited power.
You have the ability to move mountains.
You can bend rivers."

BOB ROSS, *THE JOY OF PAINTING*

I own a Bob Ross bobblehead, a Bob Ross T-shirt, and a Bob Ross board game. His long-running TV show, *The Joy of Painting*, premiered in 1983, the year I turned seven. I have never painted a landscape on canvas, but Bob Ross is so much a part of my lonely childhood memories that I truly believe that I could.

The way Bob Ross paints is predictable. There is a formula to his method: use the fewest number of strokes to suggest a tree or a mountain or a wave, and don't fuss. If you pause one of the episodes of *The Joy of Painting* and bring your face as close as possible to the screen, the swipes with his knife or the zigzags from his fan brush are just that—streaks and stamps of thick oil paint applied in as few layers as possible. There is no complexity. No subtext. Just paint arranged so that the eye is drawn to the centre of the canvas. There, a sunset. Or an angled mountaintop. Or maybe a small cottage, its roof blanketed in snow.

There have been many essays written about his voice—low, slow, steady, almost a murmur, punctuated by chuckles—and his hair, the fuzzy brown perm he maintained for the eleven years *The Joy of Painting* was on the air so as not to disrupt the consistency his viewers wanted. As I stream an episode now, I am compelled to close my eyes, the better to slip into ASMR, or autonomous sensory meridian response. My body relaxes and soon my scalp tingles, and I forget deadlines, parenting worries, and even the sounds of my dog chewing on her butt on the couch beside me. Bob Ross's voice can feel like a soothing touch without being touched.

And when I open my eyes, Bob is smiling, gently skimming his palette knife over the edges of a mountain, making planes of snow where before there was nothing, only a deep blue-black that suggests distance and rock and a cold to be protected against.

Viewers may have come to his show wanting to learn how to paint landscapes, but many of them stayed for the half-hour of calm he provided, when time hardly seemed to move. To this day, if I can't sleep, I stream an episode on my laptop and as soon as he smiles into the camera, I forget everything: the laundry piling up in the corner, the deadline I will probably miss. And finally, I sleep.

♥

My father grew up with three older sisters in a small two-room house in rural southern China, while my grandfather lived and worked in Vancouver. It wasn't until the Chinese Exclusion Act was repealed in 1947 that my father's family could apply for reunification and join my grandfather in Canada. My grandmother and aunts were strong women. They had survived Japanese occupation with no one to protect them but themselves. They could cook, clean, micro-farm, raise babies, and lecture you with disappointment dripping off every word. By the time I was born, their edges had softened just a little, and I remember making my aunties microwave popcorn and watching a romantic comedy on VHS in my family's living room, all of us giggling at every kissing scene. Still, I watched my grandmother slaughter turtles for soup, gently tapping on the shell with the handle of her cleaver until the turtle inevitably poked out his head to investigate. Then the blade would come down, a swift movement that I could barely see, and his head would be rolling across the newspaper spread on the floor.

Like my grandfather before him, my father was a gentle soul, a man who was far more comfortable being the youngest child in a household of take-charge women than he was being the head of our family. For as long as anyone can remember, our lives had been dominated by women—single mothers, older sisters, aunties who scolded as much as they loved. My maternal grandfather had three wives, and after he died when my mother was nine, her life was governed by a team of women, all of whom she called Mama, whether they were her birth mother or not. At our house, women who gave orders were what my sisters and I knew. My father would return home from work every day and often fall silent as my sisters and I fought and laughed and shouted, and as my mother grew angrier and angrier.

When I was young, my mother constantly battled the double-headed monster of anxiety and depression, sometimes loudly blaming us for everything that had gone wrong that day or that year or for her entire life, sometimes retreating to my parents' bedroom where she would stay for several days. (I think my father brought her food and water, but I'm not sure she ever consumed it.) "You," she would yell, pointing at my sisters and me as she stood at her bedroom door, "all of you. You hate me. When I die, you will all be happy."

During those times, my father did what he could: delegating chores, cooking dinner (his favourites were meatloaf with ketchup sauce, boiled corned beef and cabbage, and potato salad with hard-boiled eggs), and managing my mother's explosions of rage and sadness. If she was yelling, he tried to keep us away. If she was in bed, weeping, he brought us in, one by one, to kiss her cheek. If she was listing off the many things we had done to hurt and ruin her, he told us to line up at the foot of the bed, oldest to youngest, so we could each tell her we were sorry. Sometimes we apologized for not cleaning up after ourselves, or speaking to her in a snotty tone, or excluding her from our rapid-fire dinnertime conversations that were always in English. As the youngest, I went last and mimicked my sisters' expressions and words. My eldest sister, Wendy, was always the angriest, and she stood so straight I thought her spine might break in two from the tension. "I'm sorry," she would say, the words enunciated clearly and quickly, like bullets. Daisy spoke gently, undercurrents of fear running through her voice. Jackie was quiet, but the resentment was in her face as she stared at the floor. Penny curled her body into itself.

When it was my turn, I would say, "I'm sorry, Mama."

This ritual occurred throughout my childhood, between the ages of four and eight. Even then I knew that my mother was not being reasonable, that whatever we had done wrong in her eyes was not serious enough to warrant a reaction like this, and that not one of us felt the slightest bit sorry. According to her, there were many things we did wrong. And almost nothing we did right.

"What if I locked you out, and a scary old lady came and took you away? That would solve all of my problems," she would hiss. If I didn't finish my dinner, she would tie me to my chair with baker's twine around my ankles and left wrist until I ate every piece of food in my bowl, even if it was congealing, even if it was the liver and kidney stir-fry I hated most. More than once, after several hours, one of my sisters would secretly upend the remaining rice and meat into an unfolded paper napkin and bury the scrunched-up ball in the kitchen garbage, so that I could be set free.

My father never did this.

And he never chastised my mother for her moods, or stepped in when she was already raging. He had been surrounded by women with big personalities his whole life, yet he had no idea how to weather conflict, or express his feelings, or protect his children from his wife who often resented their existence. He knew how to hide in the garage, fiddling with a fishing rod he had been trying to build for years. He was a gifted gardener and escaped the arguments that always erupted between my mother and sisters by retreating to the backyard, where in his high rubber boots he could overturn soil and nurture his cucumbers and beans and bok choy. He was much better at making interlinguistic puns, or telling us why Tina Turner was the best entertainer of his generation, or dancing slow circles around the kitchen with his youngest daughter, pretending our family life was as peaceful as that moment, even when we both knew it wasn't, not at all.

♥

From the ages of eight to fourteen, my life is marked by a series of departures. First, it's my sister Wendy. The same year my father is diagnosed, she gets married, packs her car to the roof, and drives across the country to Toronto. Then it's my sister Jackie, who delays her wedding by six months as we plan his funeral. Last, it's my sister

Daisy, who gets married a year after Jackie and then moves to Hong Kong with her Singaporean husband. As I watch my sisters plan their weddings, pack, and leave, I note the relief written on their faces, as visible to me as their blue-lined eyes or feathered hair. They walk out the front door in new clothes and get into shiny cars driven by their new husbands, waving with wide smiles and so incandescent with contagious happiness that I find myself waving back.

My father's long illness, the funeral, the insurance, and other details—all of these things had forced my sisters and me into a tight unit for five years, the five of us often travelling as a pack to the hospital, choosing my father's funeral suit in a huddle at Moores, taking my mother for dinner so that none of us had to manage her alone. But as my older sisters left, Penny and I remained in the house, where grief was omnipresent, where our mother hovered at the periphery of our vision. Better not to engage. Better to quietly wait until we could leave too.

When my father died, Penny was not quite nineteen and just starting her second year of university. Her bedroom had been the basement kitchen; the exposed duct for the missing stove hood hovered from the ceiling above her bed, and against the opposite wall was the old teal-painted cabinet that my mother still used as her dry goods pantry. Our house had always been full, but in the aftermath of my father's death, my mother, Daisy, Jackie, Penny, and I scattered to its farthest corners, each into our own rooms, no matter what the room looked or smelled like, no matter if it was filled with boxes of mung beans and sacks of jasmine rice.

As the years passed, we learned to cocoon in our own lives whenever possible. For Penny and me, both of us still at home and many years away from starting careers or getting married, that meant finding solitary activities; I drew angrily with pastels, each piece featuring a face that looked like a sad me, even if it was only a shadowy form in a bottom corner. I could hear Penny singing in her room, often accompanying the *Les Misérables* cast recording or, sometimes, *C.M.B.* by Color Me Badd. She was a great singer, a natural alto who could reach soprano range, whose voice barrelled down the hallway and up the stairs, where I would stand at the top, so she couldn't see me, and listen.

1990 to 1995

Every Saturday morning, I wake up, eat toast with peanut butter, then rush to finish my homework before lunchtime. My mother, as she often does, stays in her room.

Shortly after noon, Penny comes up from the basement, wearing her favourite giant navy-blue sweatshirt, and lies down on the loveseat. I come out of my room and sit on the sofa, my feet propped up on the coffee table. We turn on the television to the local public station and Bob Ross appears on the screen, balancing his palette on his forearm. Today, we're lucky: it's a *Joy of Painting* marathon (he is a reliable draw, especially when the station is doing its periodic donation drives). I close my eyes as Bob lists the paint colours he'll be using in this episode: cadmium yellow, phthalo blue, titanium white.

Penny and I don't speak to each other. It's only Bob's voice drifting through the living room. "Maybe this tree needs a little friend," he says, halfway through.

A calm, masculine voice, one who only wants us to paint the best paintings we can, in this pocket of contentment. And if we never paint at all, that's okay too. On Saturday afternoons, we are both okay.

♥

My mother, who had been angry and overworked during my father's illness, withdrew further in the aftermath. On good days, she made me elaborate breakfasts with ham and eggs and hash browns. On most days, good or bad, she stayed home. Before, her friends took her for lunch when she needed a break, or drove her to Costco for the free samples of tortilla chips or chicken smokies. But now, when I arrived home after school, she was often on the couch in the living room, curtains closed against the sunlight, staring at the turned-off television. She held a balled-up tissue in her hand. Sometimes there were tears. Sometimes her face remained immobile and dry, and I wondered if it hurt more to cry or to have the tears never come.

By then, I was well used to her periods of depression. When my father was alive, they had lasted only a few days, no longer. Yet as the years wore on—as I got my period, entered high school, learned to drive, and graduated with three scholarships—her depression did not break. If she talked to me, she started crying, so I avoided her as much as possible. Once upon a time, she was a stern, raging, demanding mother, but at least she had seen me, taken note of my presence, even if I was found lacking. As I rapidly sped out of childhood and into adulthood, she was absent. She never asked where I was going or what time I would be home. She didn't know the names of most of my friends. She didn't go prom-dress shopping with me. She stayed home.

1990

Just before I turn fourteen, I need to have a new crown fitted over a chipped tooth, so my mother silently gives me a blank cheque. I take the bus downtown to the dentist's office, where he freezes my mouth and begins shaving down my tooth. By the time the drilling is done, the denturist still hasn't arrived with my brand-new crown. When my dentist calls, the denturist says she is stuck in a dental emergency and cannot leave her studio across the inlet in North Vancouver. The new crown is there and ready, but someone needs to go and get it.

My dentist looks at me and says, "Can your mom get it? I can call her in from the waiting room."

"She's not here. She's at home," I mumble, my mouth swollen.

"What? You're here alone? Who is going to drive you home?"

"I'm going to take the bus."

The dentist looks alarmed. "How will you do that? This is dental surgery!"

After a few minutes spent conferring with his receptionist and hygienist, neither of whom can leave the office, he asks, "What if I put you in a taxi, and you got the crown and came straight back? Can you do that?"

I sit up straight. "I don't need a taxi. I can take the SeaBus."

"No," he says, shaking his head. "You are not taking the SeaBus."

"I can. I'm fine. I promise."

And so I go, walking to the SeaBus terminal four blocks away. I board the little commuter ferry with cotton stuffed into the back of my mouth and get off in North Vancouver, where I walk another three blocks to the denturist's studio, located on the second floor of a warehouse just up from the train tracks. When the denturist sees me, she gasps. "Why are you here?" she asks, touching my shoulders as if to make sure I'm real.

"I came to get my crown," I say. "But can I sit down for a minute? I'm pretty tired."

"Yes, yes. Sit right here. I'm going to get you some water and we can replace that cotton."

As I rest, I can hear her talking on the phone to my dentist. She keeps asking where my parents are, why he let me take public transit by myself, who was going to drive me home. After a few minutes, she comes back.

"Jenny, if you can wait about half an hour, I'll be done, and I will drive you back downtown. And I'll drive you home afterward too."

"Oh no, no," I say, suddenly afraid of how my mother would greet this strange lady. "I can get home by myself. It's fine."

"Actually, it's not fine. I want to see you get home safely. Don't argue with me."

She drives me home, chatting the whole way about her job, about how she loves art and sculpture, how being a denturist is kind of like making art, and how happy it makes her to see her work in her patients' mouths, looking as natural as possible. I don't say much, partly because my mouth hurts, and partly because I feel calm in her presence, this woman who is only a few years younger than my mother, who loves her work, and who is kind to me even though I haven't proven that I am deserving of any kindness at all. I am just me and that is enough.

When she pulls up in front of my house, she unbuckles her seat-belt and reaches to open her door. "No," I say. "You don't have to get out. I'll just run in."

She stops and her eyes search my face, looking, I'm sure, for signs of distress or some clue as to what I am hiding. I half-expect her to insist on walking me to the front door, where she might confront my mother and ask invasive questions. But she doesn't do that. Instead, she sighs and pulls on her seatbelt again.

"Okay. Take the Tylenol the dentist gave you if it hurts too much." Then she opens the glove compartment and passes me a business card. "Call me if you need anything. Even if you just want to talk."

I stuff the card into my pocket and mutter, "Thank you." I walk up the front path and into the house. My mother, sitting on the living room sofa, doesn't say hello or ask how I am. I close the door to the bathroom, open my mouth, and pull out the last of the cotton, stained with blood, soaked with saliva, and flush it down the toilet.

♥

In a rare interview with the *Orlando Sentinel* in 1990, Bob Ross talked about his time in the U.S. Air Force: "I was the guy who makes you scrub the latrine, the guy who makes you make your bed, the guy who screams at you for being late to work. The job requires you to be a mean, tough person. And I was fed up with it. I promised myself that if I ever got away from it, it wasn't going to be that way anymore." He rehabilitated squirrels, phoned fans when he hadn't heard from them in a while to make sure they were okay, and jokingly predicted his paintings would never hang in the Smithsonian. (In 2019, several of his paintings were, in fact, donated to the Smithsonian's National Museum of American History by Bob Ross Inc., and the plan is to create a permanent exhibit on Bob, Julia

Child, and Fred Rogers.) In that same interview, he said of his appeal, "I don't intimidate anyone. Instead, I try to get people to believe in themselves. I tell people, 'You can do this.' And they write back and say, 'You were right. I can do this. And now I believe I can do anything.'"

♥

There was a hole to be filled in my adolescence and this, perhaps, was the biggest problem with the grief that took over my family in those years. My three oldest sisters had found whole other worlds in which to exist, to find love, to be valued. Penny and I weren't there yet, and the care my father took with us was gone, with nothing to take its place.

When my school wanted to skip me ahead one full grade, my father had asked me what I wanted. I said no, I wanted to stay with my friends, and he allowed me to stay where I was. When the two of us were out shopping for Penny's birthday, he asked if she would like a dark blue denim jacket. "No," I said, "this one." I pointed to an oversized acid-washed jacket. He listened and bought it, and it was the jacket Penny wore for years, long after his death.

As he was painting his landscapes, Bob Ross would often say, "You make the decisions in this world." And then he would paint a mountain where nothing had existed before. Or a rock. Or a cloud tinged with pink. Bob could make entire worlds out of paint and canvas, and every Saturday we tried to fill our own emptiness with his smile, his voice, his resolute belief that we would all be okay.

1992

My father kept his legal papers and special photographs in an old desk, varnished yellow. It had been used by my sisters when they were little, and it is short and narrow, perched on the spindly wooden legs that mark furniture made in the middle of the twentieth century. The drawer pulls are brass buttons, small enough to fit in between two fingers. It still sits in a corner of our parents' bedroom, now only my mother's, near the door to the ensuite bathroom.

Penny and I are looking for my father's high school yearbooks, to see what he looked like when he idolized Jerry Lee Lewis and smoked American cigarettes. In the bottom drawer of that little yellow desk, we find photographs from his early days in Vancouver's Chinatown, when he was a teenaged boy who carried his portable radio everywhere he went. There are old letters, written in Chinese, folded neatly into thin envelopes, addresses faded to barely there blue. At the very bottom, we find a sketchbook, its binding falling apart. Penny opens it slowly.

My father's sketches fill the pages. Landscapes, with towering evergreen trees. Cityscapes, with sidewalks and storefronts. And near the end, portraits of my mother as a young woman, drawings she must have posed for. In one, drawn in pencil with light lines, my mother is nude and in a reclining position. She floats—there is no furniture, no floor. Just her, the page around her untouched.

We have never seen this sketchbook before. It lies open, cracking at the edges, and I touch the lines he has drawn with my finger. They are so light, the paper perfectly smooth.

Once, my father was an artist. Once, my mother's brain was quiet enough that it allowed her to pose, unashamed, unmoored in an ocean of calm.

1994

The summer has just started and the air is warm and humid, the kind of air that traps sweat on skin. My mother travels to Singapore, where my sister Daisy is living with her husband and infant son. She leaves me, eighteen years old, and Penny, twenty-five, alone, although we haven't been under her care for years. Her absence only matters because, with her away, a shadow lifts off the house. Penny and I play music at all hours—Barenaked Ladies and the Tragically Hip for me, Broadway show tunes for her. I plan a high school graduation party and invite most of my class. I buy four-litre buckets of ice cream and boxes of Old Dutch chips.

Penny and her boyfriend arrive home from a dinner out and walk up the front steps where drunk teenagers are sitting silently, waiting to get in trouble. She laughs instead and greets me with "This looks fun." They retreat to the basement and lock the door; my friends and I take over the main floor again. By the time the police arrive, my friend Neil has shown up wearing green hospital scrubs and with a case of beer, and my oldest friend Ronni is engaged in a shouting match with her ex-boyfriend's new girlfriend. As the two women emerge from their cruiser, drunk and high teenagers are hiding bottles in the potted plants and flushing joints down the toilet. I am crying noisily before the officers even say a word.

The next morning, Penny walks up the stairs from the basement and helps me clean up the ice cream that has melted all over the kitchen counters, the beer caps strewn across the lawn, while gingerly stepping around the three sleeping girls on the living room floor. She pulls down the banner I had hung on the top shelf in the dining room, where it obscured the funeral portraits of my father and grandparents. In painted block letters, it shouts JEN'S MOM IS OUT OF TOWN. In daylight, the joke isn't as funny.

In the afternoon, we sit down in our newly cleaned living room. Bob Ross is on TV, and I fall asleep somewhere in the middle of the episode. When I wake up, Penny is gone, but she has tucked a blanket around me and left a glass of water on the side table.

1995

Penny has been busy, working at an administration job at the University of British Columbia, where I am finishing my first year in a multidisciplinary arts program. Every Monday afternoon, I ostentatiously read *The Second Sex* or *The Wealth of Nations* in the student pub with a pint of beer that I never really drink. Penny and I carpool together in the mornings, and by February, she begins to tell me about her burgeoning plan on our long drive from the easternmost part of Vancouver to its very western edge.

"I'm going to move out, Jen. Help me figure it out."

So far, the only acceptable way for my sisters to leave home is to hold a traditional Chinese wedding to an acceptable Chinese man, before they turn thirty. Penny has no man she is serious about and she is, at twenty-six, restless. Every evening, she runs around the track at the local high school, circles and circles that lead nowhere, until she is shaking and thirsty and returns home, where she peels an orange while looking at the North Shore mountains through the window.

Her apartment is nothing special, a basement suite in a nearby suburb, not unlike where Penny currently sleeps. The setting is unremarkable, but the symbolism isn't.

This is what we come up with as we drive fifty minutes to campus every morning: two weeks before she is supposed to move, she will bring her new roommate to dinner, a Chinese girl not so different from us. The roommate has excellent Cantonese skills and my mother will be charmed by her manners and pretty face. The conversation will be nice. My mother will be social, offering seconds to our guest.

And this is the way it goes, until Penny tells her. "We rented an apartment, Mom. I'm moving out."

Her roommate nods and smiles, but her dimples aren't working on my mother anymore.

She goes still and silent. After several minutes, she asks one question: "Why are you leaving me?"

Penny stumbles through an answer. "It's not about leaving you, Mom. It's about living my own life. About being an adult and growing up."

"You're unmarried. I am so ashamed. All of my daughters just want to shame me."

Penny has nothing to say in reply. I stare down at my rice bowl. Somehow the silence is both better and worse than I had feared.

When my mother stands up and walks to her bedroom, it's a relief. The air she leaves behind is filled with disappointments like small bombs detonating one after the other, but at least the break has been made. Penny has tears in her eyes, but the release is better than numbness.

♥

Grief is both nonsensical and practical. It pushes us to find distractions like boyfriends or fashion magazines or books, things we can pile up around the hole that's been left behind, so we can forget, for moments or days, that we're sad, that an essential part of us is missing. Sometimes the distractions don't help at all, only crumble away into dust, leaving you with nothing to do but stare at the gaping grief straight on. The hole remains, partially hidden maybe, but it's always there. For Penny and me, ours was the shape of our father, a tall thin man with big hands and tinted aviator glasses, who liked to spit cherry pits over the railing of our deck, sometimes clearing our station wagon parked below, often not. It was a hole so specific, so deeply carved out of our bodies and brains, we flailed through those after years, trying—and failing—to move forward in our limited worlds.

I wish I remembered the last time Penny and I watched *The Joy of Painting* together. It's a memory I could make up, paint with the details I would wish for, rather than the ones that really occurred. Maybe we shared a bowl of salt and vinegar chips. Maybe we made plans for sister dinners together, or complained about our summertime boyfriends who disappeared when September was imminent. Maybe we told each other, "I love you," as Bob Ross used a fluffy brush to paint fluffy white clouds. Maybe he said, "You have to allow the paint to break to make it beautiful."

What I do remember is that after Penny moved out, I never watched *The Joy of Painting* in my mother's house again. Bob Ross was specific to the grief Penny and I had been trying to manage in our adolescence and young adulthood, and then she had left, with a job and suitcases and men to date. I missed her like I had never missed anyone before, not even my other sisters. This was a whole other loss, one that I felt acutely all day long. In the mornings, I was reminded that we used to drive to campus together. At dinnertime, she used to fill my rice bowl with a smile. On Saturday afternoons, I always knew when *The Joy of Painting* was on and could not bear the thought of watching it alone. But at least now I had my own departure to plan. And every day brought me closer to leaving.

♥

Bob Ross has been called many things since *The Joy of Painting* was first broadcast. People have criticized his art for being kitschy and formulaic, his presentation manner a form of pandering bad art to the masses. He has also been called an icon and an American treasure, his position in the memories of thousands akin to sainthood. Bob Ross Inc. maintains a toll-free number, 1-800-BOB-ROSS, and many of the calls they receive are from fans who want to tell them how much Bob has changed their lives.

My memories of my father have been suffused with a dreamy perfection, like an Instagram filter of the mind. He was funny and kind and did his best to give each of his daughters individual attention. He made very good sandwiches. If I remember his flaws at all, it's only when I force myself to do so. He was weak-willed and conflict-avoidant, a man who would turtle in a corner rather than face an interaction he was dreading. His favourite pants were red-and-grey plaid bell bottoms that everyone else hated.

Bob and my father both loved art, as many people do, but they loved art without worrying over their greatness as artists. It didn't matter if that landscape looked like every other landscape. It didn't matter that a sketch was never fully realized, that the lines were shaky or details like hands or flowers were purposefully obscured to cover a lack of skill. They had jobs: father, business partner, husband, de facto therapist. To be an artist in the classical sense may have been their goal when they were young, but as life marched on, art took on another role. Art helped them understand the world around them. Art helped them to make a coherent narrative out of the mess of their lives.

Bob was a former Air Force master sergeant, a man who never put people in his paintings, only rivers and shrubs and mountains. He was from central Florida, had a drawl that was long and slow, and wore his shirts unbuttoned to his chest hair. He used to paint land-scapes on gold pans and sell them to tourists in Alaska for money. His pet rescue squirrel was named Peapod.

My father combed pomade through his hair every morning, kept a snow globe with a miniature version of Toronto's CN Tower on his desk, and cut grocery-store coupons out of flyers and newspapers with my mother every Friday night. He joked they would retire to Salt Spring Island, where he would install a kiln and grow his hair long to fit in. His dream car was a silver Mercury Sable.

Bob told us we were okay, that our lives were not mistakes but happy little accidents. He told us that the first step toward finishing anything was to believe we could.

The last thing my father ever said to me was "You're smart enough to do whatever you want. Or maybe not. Maybe you just have a smart mouth." And then he leaned back in his hospital bed and giggled, eyes closed with the delight of his small joke, as I held his thin shivering hand.

THE
GOOD PRINCESS

Type this into your search engine: "Diana and Charles wedding." You will see a long list of video hits, many more hits than you will ever have time to watch. Click on the first or the second or the twelfth. They are all mostly the same anyway.

♥

It's 1981, a cloudy July day. Diana Spencer is in a horse-drawn carriage, only her veil and tiara visible through the glass of the window. When the carriage arrives at St. Paul's Cathedral, she emerges and stands still on the steps outside, as women and girls smooth and fluff her silk taffeta skirt and straighten her twenty-five-foot train. When the camera zooms in on Diana's face, her tiara—a Spencer family heirloom—catches the light and glitters, even in the grey London mist.

She waves. She smiles. She whispers a joke to her father. If she is scared or tentative or feeling any doubt at all, she is hiding it spectacularly well. She is not exactly demure. She is charming, tall, graceful in a dress with layers of crinoline and ivory ruffles. But not shy.

I am not quite five, and even though I'm groggy from being woken up in the middle of the night by my sisters to sit in front of the small TV in the basement, I can't help but stare and think, *Shiny. She's so shiny*. I think I love her. My sisters chatter about her dress, her makeup, the cream and white and yellow flowers in her cascading bouquet, all of it coming to us through a camera, then a satellite dish, then our slightly greenish, flickering screen. I hear them but I don't. The light from the TV is magnetic, or maybe it's Diana's light, somehow perfect for drawing in little Chinese girls lying on the floor of a family room in East Vancouver.

Oh, I love her, I decide. *I really, really do.*

♥

The year before she got married, Lady Diana Spencer was nineteen years old and working as an assistant kindergarten teacher in London. Her relationship with Prince Charles was still new, and her identity unknown to the public, until one sunny fall day when paparazzi photographers caught her taking her students to a public park. The resulting image—of an unsmiling and fresh-faced young woman balancing one child on her hip while holding the hand of another, backlit by afternoon sunshine, her legs plainly visible through her thin cotton skirt—is visual gold.

She was all the things my sisters and I were supposed to aspire to back then: pretty but not flashy, devoted to children, well-mannered enough to be acceptable to a prince and, most importantly, his mother. And yet there is a glimmer of defiance. She is standing with her legs apart, light filtering through her skirt. Diana was a lady, and the girlfriend of a prince, yet she did not wear a slip, or practical trousers, or hose of any kind. Maybe she saw the photographers waiting outside her bedroom window that morning; maybe she didn't. Maybe when she dressed, she knew the day would be humid, as warm days in London can be. Maybe she just didn't care.

My sisters and I saw in this photograph the promise of subversion. As good Chinese girls, we had learned a particular way of moving through the world. We walked down sidewalks hugging the walls of buildings as much as possible, keeping distance between our bodies and the possibly angry, potentially racist people that could be anywhere. We drove to church as a group—Wendy driving my father's station wagon—and then drove straight back home. We experimented with makeup and curling irons only in the safety of our house, where we were our only audience. If my sisters wore their lavender lipstick or candy-coloured pumps in public, they had to sneak out first, running out the door with their backs to our parents, heads down, faces hidden by hair, high heels in their purses. Their boyfriends were from church or school and knew to address my parents as Aunty and Uncle.

Upon their arrivals in Canada, my parents and grandparents had discovered that their visibility as Chinese immigrants did not help when they applied for a job or visited a government office or tried to buy a car. They came to believe that invisibility—achieved only if you never got into trouble—was the right, if not ideal, way to survive with their bodies and livelihoods intact. They became model citizens, buying into the model minority myth because the other options— poverty, ridicule, victimization—were real and looming threats. In North America, there is a hierarchy of race, as determined by whiteness and power, and the last thing my parents and grandparents wanted was to fall down that ladder and expose my sisters and me to virulent racism, violence, and dead ends. During the first half of the twentieth century, my family didn't realize that they were serving the needs of white supremacy; these were conversations that my sisters and I would only have sixty years later. Back then, my family saw one road to survival and took it.

My grandfather, once a gifted calligraphist, owned a barbershop. My father, who sketched in a notebook when no one was looking, was an accountant. My mother, who dreamed about singing onstage like Doris Day, made the best cream puffs anyone had ever tasted. They chose what caused the least amount of trouble.

Above all else, they wanted my sisters and me to be *safe*. No makeup, no patting stray dogs, no boyfriends, no sleepovers. Performing well at school was a way to ensure future safety. Attending church was a way to keep busy and protected from risk. Sewing your own ill-fitting clothes hid your body. No one lost track of girls who were on the honour roll, taught Sunday school, and wore homemade pants with crotches that were too long. (In a rare spurt of rebellion, I pierced the upper cartilage on my right ear three times during my final year of high school. My mother noticed while we were eating dinner, threw down her chopsticks, and cried, "Are you one of those people who sits at the *back of the bus*?")

We were the girls who were going to have stable careers, marry men who did not hurt us, and raise children who cared for us in our old age, in our own homes.

And in 1981, we were on track for all of that. Wendy had just finished her undergraduate degree in microbiology and was working in a lab. Daisy was entering her first year at university. Jackie was still in high school and spent every Friday night styling our hair in the safety of our kitchen, one sister at a time. Penny, at eleven years old, was already a gifted singer and visual artist. And me? At five, I had already learned to read, and my parents were struggling to find ways to rein in my busy, restless brain. "You'll make a good lawyer one day," my father said. "You like to talk back."

Being a woman, especially a woman of colour, meant that life was always a long game. You worked hard. You kept your reputation clean. You waited for your opportunities. And then, one day, maybe you could be who you wanted. My entire childhood and adolescence I wrote poems and stories, which my father read and enjoyed, but I never told him, or anyone else, that my greatest wish was to be a writer. I was on track to go to law school and I was willing to bide my time, to wait for the moment when this choice, being a writer, would seem safe enough. Even then, I knew I might have to wait for midlife, when I had six weeks of paid vacation to write, or even later, when I was retired and living in a nice waterfront condo and needed something to fill my time.

It's hard to know if Diana knew she was being photographed that day. Here, in the afternoon light, she is doing her job, wrangling small children while they play outdoors. And yet her eyes are not looking at her students, her mouth isn't open to shout at them from across the park. Her expression is composed and still and turned in the right direction for the right light.

I think she knew. And I think she had something to say.

That skirt, transparent in broad daylight, and her bare, uncompromising legs were forecasting the future, or at least messaging to the world that she was not the sort of woman to wear a lined tweed suit and never would be. In 1980, she was already telling us that, already revealing the woman she would become in the body of the girl she would very shortly leave behind.

A year later, Diana was married and on her way to one day becoming queen. It was done. She was safe. As long as she didn't fuck it up.

♥

Respectability for Chinese women is a complicated knot, one that has its origins in history, in Confucianism, in migration, in popular culture. My sisters and I, and many Chinese women who grew up in North America, were raised to believe that there is one way to stay safe, and that is to be good. If you're nice and polite, the next time a drunk man in a bar hisses that he saw a girl just like you on Pornhub, another man will step in and push him away. If you're pretty but not too sexy, the police officer will wave your car through a check stop, even if you've had a few cocktails. If you have good grades, no one will ever suspect your boyfriend is a gangster.

But if you're bad, there are no guarantees. Your family could disown you. A white man could rape you and no one would believe you. You might never graduate high school and have to work in a nail salon in a strip mall, scraping the feet of women who think they're better than you. You will bring shame to your parents. This, by far, is the worst of all outcomes.

My oldest sisters, who spent the five years of my father's illness managing the medical and legal details that my mother couldn't, must have felt as if they had never had choices, that they had been chained to the responsibilities of their Chinese daughterhood without reprieve. Chinese culture is built upon the centrality of the family, on families taking care of their members, on families making decisions for the collective, not the individual. In most dialects of Chinese, no one addresses their family members by name, only by their position in the family: mother, father, oldest sister, fourth maternal aunt. Who you are isn't important. What you do in the family is all that matters, and those roles are rigidly defined, both in title and in function.

In traditional Chinese households, the women, who are most often the caregivers and the homemakers, have very little opportunity outside of the home. If a family has only enough money to send one of their children to school, who will they send: the son, who will always earn more and work longer, or the daughter, who could get pregnant and never earn a consistent income? In our family of all daughters and no sons, the weight was doubly heavy. We had to be good enough to get respectable jobs and marry a man who brought the family more than he took away. We had to make up for our feminine limitations by being better than everyone—the boys, the other girls, the pretty kid down the street who was a figure skating champion and a straight-A student all at the same time. One misstep might lead to another, until the mistakes piled up and buried us alive.

But there were five of us and only so much righteousness to go around. It was only a matter of time. One of us was going to fail.

♥

It's the dress, isn't it, that fascinates you now, forty years later, as you stare at your screen. The balloon sleeves, the ruffled neck, the almost certainly boned bodice that holds Diana, who had a tendency to slouch, as many tall women do, straight and stiff and smooth. You wish you could run your fingers along the silk, feel the weave—or the luxurious lack of weave—as the fabric shimmers under a bright light, a special light to illuminate every mark that could not be erased, every wrinkle that could not be steamed. Nothing is ever as spotless as it seems, especially now, after so much time has passed, after you have learned things about what Diana wanted, what she pushed against, what she valued, and what she threw away.

You are no longer five years old, wrapped in an old blanket, bum on the shag carpet, watching a tiny Diana smile benevolently at her attendants who fuss over the folds of her veil. You are a grown-ass woman who can almost hear the beginnings of a fire—of baby flames licking at elitist, rigid, royal kindling—that was surely already growing inside Diana. You are familiar with the sound. The same kind of fire has been licking at your insides for as long as you can remember.

Now it's so very obvious. That dress—that many-layered, steel-trapped, rigorously structured dress—was designed to suffocate as much as it was to entertain.

♥

In August of 1997, I turned twenty-one years old. To celebrate, my girlfriends from high school and I planned a trip: we were going to borrow a Dodge Caravan and drive down the coast to Los Angeles and then inland to Las Vegas. Before I told my mother about our plans, I had worried she would try to stop me. I saw the road trip as a precursor to my escape from her house, which was slowly taking shape in my brain, so I stood straight, body tensed, ready for her to burst into rage and say I was ungrateful, that the loneliness might kill her. But she said nothing. She just gave me an envelope of American cash to spend. I thought I should hug her, but she turned and walked away, and I was left alone in the kitchen, back slouched. Still, I left on a high of optimism.

On our way from L.A. to Las Vegas, the van started smoking through the gas pedal, causing my best friend Ronni, who was driving, to yell, "Is my foot on fire?!" We stopped in the middle of the night at the only rest stop between Barstow and the city, and were swarmed by bats, which dive-bombed our heads while we huddled at a phone booth, trying to find a way to get towed to Circus Circus, the hotel I had booked because I had read *Fear and Loathing in Las Vegas* twice that summer and had decided any hotel that was weird enough for Hunter S. Thompson was weird enough for us.

Stuck in Las Vegas for three extra days while our van was repaired, we haunted hotel lobbies for cheap buffets and clean bathrooms. At the Venetian, we saw Michael Jordan stride into the back of the glitzy casino, where he disappeared through a pair of double doors that closed behind him with a whisper. At the Mirage, Ronni played blackjack against a trio of boys from Harvard and won. We drank watered-down margaritas at the nickel slots and ventured outside only at night to avoid the oppressive heat. It was an untethered, surreal time. When we received the call that the van was fixed, we were itching to just get home.

We left our hotel the afternoon of August 31 and wasted no time speeding down the desert highway. We stopped for water, food, gas, and toilets, sometimes brushing our teeth in service station bathrooms, sometimes not bothering. Afraid our van would break down again, we didn't turn on the air conditioning and fell asleep with our heads at right angles, pressed against the rubbery interior, only to wake up in pools of our own sweat that had collected under our cheeks. That night, the highway was pitch-black, and we drove with NPR turned up loud, reasoning that if we were going to return to real life, then we should know what had been happening outside of the twenty-four-hour climate-controlled casinos.

A man's voice cut through the air: "We have breaking news." His solemn tone was alarming. I had been dozing in the middle row and sat up straight. Ronni turned up the volume. "We have received a report that Princess Diana has been involved in a car accident and has died in Paris. We are still waiting to confirm, but it appears that, again, Princess Diana has died at the age of thirty-six."

We were silent for a minute, Ronni fiddling with the volume dial as if she could fix this announcement that seemed so totally wrong. Finally, a friend in the back yelled into the darkness, "What?!"

Outside, the desert was unseeable, obliterated by the night, the stars not bright enough to illuminate anything beyond themselves. We continued driving into the dark.

I cried, the tears big and silent, running down my face, the same face that had sweated during our hours-long drive through the Mojave Desert. I remembered that photograph of Diana on a roller coaster with her sons, laughing as if nothing else mattered. I remembered her wedding, the puffed sleeves that made her seem more fairy-like and insubstantial than she ever really was. And I remembered that first scandalous public photograph and her legs in silhouette, a harbinger of her rebellious desire to recast her princess role. In the years that followed, she became a princess like none who had come before.

According to Diana, when she confronted Camilla Parker Bowles about her affair with Charles, Camilla's response was "You've got everything you've ever wanted. All the men in the world fall in love with you. You have two beautiful children. What more would you want?" Diana replied, "I want my husband." This conversation has always made my heart hurt.

Diana had what the world had scripted for her. She was a beautiful, high-born woman who looked good in a tiara and ballgown. She loved a prince who did not love her back; during the course of her marriage, she did what was expected of her. She gave birth to two princes. She didn't make a fuss. Camilla's assumption of what Diana wanted was not necessarily what Diana had dreamed for herself, but rather what the world had trained her to believe was the right way to achieve security, respectability, and happiness. As it turned out, Diana wanted other things. Romance. Charity. Glamour. Maybe some drama too. After her divorce and before her death, it seemed, at least for a short time, she got what she wanted. She sat on the prow of her wealthy boyfriend's yacht in a swimsuit, feet dangling above the Mediterranean. A real, individual, and distinctly unroyal moment caught in a paparazzi photograph.

On that night in August, I was just starting to figure out what my adult life was going to be. Within three months, I met the man I would go on to marry and then divorce. I was plotting to escape my mother's house by moving to Montreal to attend graduate school, not for law but for creative writing. I had already put in twenty-one years as a good Chinese girl. I knew how to make a perfect pot of rice. I had finished Cantonese school and piano lessons. I had won scholarships that paid for my entire undergrad. I was done. I had already decided that I would become the person I wanted to be at my new school, in my own apartment, in a different city. That person would order the right wine at dinner, smoke clove cigarettes perched on a fire escape, and perform poems in a bar with red velvet chairs.

Diana had escaped a marriage bound by restrictions, rules, and protocols, and a manufactured persona that had barely evolved since the monarchy began.

I was not a princess, or even a girl from an established family, and yet my own escape felt vital, as I imagined Diana's must have felt. The restlessness—the anxious desire to keep moving—that I first felt in my childhood did not go away. Instead, it pushed me farther and farther, to Montreal and beyond, because I knew, at twenty-one, that there were possibilities beyond what others had prescribed. Diana had shown me. I had been watching her my entire life.

♥

Wendy had a career in marketing that spanned thirty years, and then she went back to school to get her Ph.D., which she now uses to teach business students at a university in England. She is still married to her first boyfriend. Daisy was an executive headhunter in Hong Kong and Singapore, before switching gears in her late forties to become a counselling psychologist. Jackie worked as a bookkeeper and then opened up her own modern furniture store, which fills the condos of tech executives and Instagram influencers. Penny, after singing in choirs and bands, started her own parenting magazine and now manages communications for a technical university. All of their children are polite, accomplished, and educated.

My father told me once I was smart enough to be the prime minister. My mother said I was the one who had an instinctive talent for cooking. I was outgoing. I made friends easily. From kindergarten to university, I was on the honour roll every single year. My high school English teacher wrote a reference letter that called me a "future literary superstar."

I never finished my graduate program. I lied about wanting to be a lawyer. I was boy-crazy. I cut all my hair off. I wore low-cut tops. I drank. I got married too young. I wrote poems no one ever read. I still couldn't stand up straight. I waited ten years to get pregnant. I got divorced. I got divorced. I got divorced. I lost it all.

Maybe our family's respectability was wrung dry after four daughters. Or maybe the fifth just wasn't built for it.

I was the failure in the family. Starting in my twenties, my mother told me so, over and over again, the frequency increasing every year until it reached its peak when my marriage was irrevocably over, when I was signing the mortgage papers on my townhouse, so much smaller than the hundred-year-old house we used to own.

"I am ashamed of you," she said, "because you have never done anything right."

It didn't occur to her that maybe, just maybe, I never wanted to.

♥

It's been more than twenty-five years since Diana's death. Her sons, William and Harry, are adults with wives and children of their own. Harry married Meghan Markle, a divorced American actress who, once she was living within the confines of royal life, saw precisely what made the princess role a gilded prison, as Diana had experienced before her. Unlike Diana though, Meghan is Black and carries with her the ability to see privilege more clearly, to see through the romance and pomp and analyze the rules of behaviour for what they are: a system of privilege that only benefits the very few.

When Meghan grew unhappy with the reality of being a princess—with the racist headlines in the British tabloids and the reluctance of the royal family to speak up for her as she increasingly became a target—she and Harry decided to leave their royal titles and England behind and move to California. It's not hard to see Harry, who would never be king anyway, as an active participant in this decision. His mother, as he and the rest of the world knows, was desperately unhappy with her marriage and confined life, as Meghan became. Diana left the princess life on her own. Meghan followed the same path but took her princely husband with her. Diana, I think, would have approved.

♥

My mother—who was once a Hong Kong debutante, who wore corsets at night to whittle her waistline to twenty-four inches, who always posed for photographs with her legs crossed at the ankles—was afraid. The possibilities for disaster were endless, but she knew one way to stay safe. *Be good. Keep your head down. Don't make trouble.* And so she moved to Canada to escape Communist China. She gave birth to daughter after daughter while trying for a boy—a boy who would have had an uninterrupted career and ensured a nice retirement for his parents, a boy who would never be born. She nursed her husband with teas and soups from the herbalist, ran an Epsom salt bath for him every night to stave off the creeping, growing cancer. And at forty-nine, she became a widow, a single mother with no job and minimal English skills.

My mother, with her anxious, circling brain, must have gone back in time over and over, during those days when she didn't move from the living room couch, those nights when she locked herself in her room. She must have looked for the one thing she could have done better, that would have changed the course of events so that her husband—the one she thought represented the safest, most prudent life—would be sleeping beside her still, waking her up in the mornings with his silly puns and off-key singing of Jerry Lee Lewis songs. Maybe she should have cut back on his beef intake, thrown away his packs of cigarettes, or gone jogging with him in the evenings. Maybe he should have gone to bed earlier. Maybe she could have been more patient as she waited for him to fix the basement fridge.

How she must have hated it when I became a single mother too. She knew how hard, how unstable, this path could be. She saw how my life was unfolding—very much like hers.

♥

In the end, Diana left behind the future king and some respectability. She admitted to an affair. She told her story. She gambled on a womanizing businessman. She also advocated publicly and volubly for HIV and AIDS patients, walked through a minefield in Angola to shine a light on post-conflict dangers, and visited homeless shelters in London, all causes that were deeply rooted in the experiences of being human, and distinctly unroyal. In 1995, three years after her separation, she famously said, "I would like a monarchy that has more contact with its people." No longer under the supervision of the Queen or Charles, Diana modelled that contact, but it wasn't really for herself, as she was no longer an official member of the royal family. She was planning ahead, for the day when her sons would take on their adult roles, roles that, following her example, have shifted to charity work, something both William and Harry are committed to. These were her post-marriage choices and her legacy, and they led to the world understanding that princesses—no matter how beautiful, no matter how polite—are not perfect, and have voices, opinions, and goals.

The day I told my mother about my separation, I had to repeat myself three times. She could not understand, or she was choosing not to.

"He seemed to love you," she said. "Didn't he? Doesn't he still?"

"Maybe he does. I don't know."

"But he makes good money. He takes care of you. My friends, everyone says he is a catch. *Why would you do this?*"

I had no real answer, only the certainty that our marriage was over, that there was a future ahead of me that was totally mine, that if I had to be alone, in a smaller house and thrifted clothes, I could make it work. But this is not what I said.

"I guess we were fighting a lot," I replied. But it was only half-true.

Afterward, after all the finances and custody had been settled, joy crept in, slowly at first but then in explosions, one after the other. The launch of my third novel. The day I moved into my townhouse. Drinking beer and eating snacks at a pub with new writer friends over Christmas. Playing with my son on a Thai beach on our first vacation alone. Meeting a date at a happy hour, where I made him eat a Scotch egg. Picking up my rescue dog at the airport, her small body wiggling in my lap as if I had known her forever. Had I followed the respectability script, none of that would have happened.

During this period of almost two years, my mother and I did not speak, not at family parties, not on the phone. She came to the book prize gala where I was a finalist but did not meet my eye or congratulate me. She told my sisters she was embarrassed of me and that anything I said or did only made her feel despair and humiliation and worry. To my mother, I was the family failure, the one who had slipped through the cracks of her carefully planned life, who ended up just as she had—alone with a dwindling bank account—but shamefully, through divorce.

"She's always mad at one of us," Penny said, when she called to ask about the obvious conflict. "It's just your turn now. Enjoy the silence."

♥

Normally, to fill silence you have to speak, and act. But you find the quiet is foundational and fertile, and you can feel your own wants beating with every contraction of your heart: *I want, I want, I want.* When the external voice that usually blankets you in its fear or its blame falls away, your own voice—your long-held desires, your secret potential future—fills the vacuum. At first, it feels like a punishment: the classic silent treatment. But then you realize that what you feel deep inside your body is actually relief. Finally, your spine is released from being held so straight because someone was always watching.

Finally, you breathe in and your chest expands, taking up as much of the space around you as possible. Finally, in the mirror, it's only you, and not your transparent face with someone else's thoughts within.

Now you know this to be true: Diana was never really all that good in the first place. And neither were you.

THE
BOYS ON FILM

The mornings after are always the hardest. You are a single mother, lonely six nights out of seven. When your child-free night arrives, you drink one, two, three glasses of wine quickly, to get you where you have to be to forget that you never have enough money, that your ex is getting remarried, that the only human who has touched you in weeks is your child, his hands sticky with filial need. You sing-shout to the music in a crowded bar, in a crop top and fake leather pants. An improbably handsome reclaimed-wood carpenter asks, "Did you grow up white?" It's a nonsensical question, but you know what he means. He wants to know if your childhood home smelled funny, if your father worked in Hong Kong while your mother raised you in a stucco box in an ethnic enclave, if you drive a champagne-coloured Lexus, if your favourite childhood actor was Leslie Cheung. Instead of throwing your gin and tonic in his face and calling him the racist that he is, you shrug and say, "Sure, I guess so."

Months later, he will tell you he can't see you anymore because there is a girl back home, in small-town Ontario, who still loves him. You find out later that they grew up together, that her hair falls in beachy waves, that she knows how to start a bonfire when they go to the lake, that she has a name that only white girls have—the Ashleys, the Siobhans, the Kristens or Kirstens or Kierstens. He offers to come over anyway, but you say no. You call someone else, who arrives in forty-five minutes, the scent of his body wash disguising the fact that you don't like him all that much.

The morning after, you look at your body in the mirror, small and straight and thin. You bruise easily and you wince when you press a finger into the blue traces he has left on your thighs. God, you hate yourself. This shower had better be hot as fuck.

♥

I remember when I first heard about the writer Evelyn Lau. It was 1989, and she had just published her first book, *Runaway: Diary of a Street Kid*, a bestselling memoir of her teenaged years when she ran away from her Chinese Canadian parents, immigrants who yearned so desperately for the success of their children that they were unable to accept Evelyn's individual needs and ambitions. She wanted to write poetry, to live freely in a body that her mother repeatedly said was fat, to express emotions without the fear of punishment. As she moves from street to shelter to couch, she is broken by abuse and predators. Yet she is also broken open, revealing the self she had been forced to hide from her parents. She writes of sex work, addiction, identity, and poetry, always poetry.

Evelyn was giving an interview on the evening news, which my sisters and I always turned on, even though the only person in our family who had ever cared about the news was my father, and he had died the previous year. Still, it was a habit, something we could do to fill the silence that his absence and my mother's depression had created.

Evelyn, then eighteen, was poised on camera, with an aura of calm that belied her age. But her face was young, rounded at the jaw and cheeks, much like mine and my sisters'. Her flat nose, her permed hair, the black eyeliner—it was all so familiar. Evelyn looked like every Chinese girl we knew, except she had run away from home, as no good Chinese girl would ever do, and written a book about it.

Halfway through the interview, they cut from Evelyn to footage of her parents hurrying down a rainy sidewalk in what looked like the East Vancouver neighbourhood where we lived. The houses were small square bungalows, the fences were chain-linked, the cars were plain functional Toyotas and Fords. The reporter followed Mr. and Mrs. Lau, asking them a series of questions, one after another.

"Are you proud of your daughter's accomplishments?"

"Is it true that she ran away because you wouldn't allow her to write poems?"

"Did you know she was living on the streets?"

"Is there anything you want to say to her?"

I remember the shots of the two of them, heads down in the rain, moving as a unit and saying nothing. I thought I could see fear in their bodies, hunched over in thin raincoats made of the kind of fabric that repelled water for only a short time before darkening as the drops seeped in.

My sisters were horrified. Over dinner that night, we talked about nothing else.

"Why didn't she just wait until she was eighteen before she left home?"

"Did you see how sad her parents looked?"

"Who doesn't have mean Chinese parents? Should we all run away and become hookers?"

The dark side of Evelyn's story was undeniable. The sex work, the group homes, the drugs—the layers to all of this were unfathomable to me at thirteen; they were simply disasters that needed to be avoided at all costs. I didn't know much about sex work, or how public perceptions of sex workers and their agency are often at odds with the truth of their lives. I didn't know about the intersections between addiction and mental illness and race and gender, or how invisibly and expendably sex workers are treated in our culture.

For me, the revolutionary idea was that Evelyn was a writer, a *poet*. And she had written a book. A real printed and bound book. She had run away with nothing but her notebooks and a restless mind that demanded she write during every quiet moment. I had been hiding in books for years by then, writing stories and poetry that circled around children who battled witches and monsters, who faced their own deaths and survived; children whose families faded into the background because the child, almost always a girl, had places to go and adventures to begin. My writing was sad, the poems containing lines that started with the everyday and drifted into loss, always loss. "The renewed summer opened quietly," I wrote, "and my father remained in my mind, buried underneath the junk of my life. Even before he died, I'd killed him."

Evelyn had tried to live intensely, to be an artist, to be free in a way that transcended the mundane lives of her Chinese immigrant parents. Her parents were like my parents, like the parents of so many kids I knew growing up in East Vancouver, where every house contained a family from another place—Fiji, Italy, the Philippines.

They were the working poor, struggling to make ends meet at their jobs at the produce market, the mechanic's garage on Kingsway, the chicken processing plant a few blocks west. They were, understandably, fixated on tangible financial successes. Jobs that put food on the table and paid the mortgage. Jobs that could be bragged about. Jobs that eased them into peaceful old age. Poetry as a vocation was the exact opposite of that. Poetry was the artful and deliberate manipulation of words to say exactly what you wanted. It was a pinnacle, a way of showing that you had surpassed the multicultural dream and mastered the English language in a way your parents and grandparents never could, in a way that a respectable doctor or lawyer might only dream about when they had a minute to remember their irresponsible childhood ambitions. But there would never be money to be made in writing it.

And yet the only thing I knew for sure was that I wanted to publish books, and that I wanted someone to see the value in my poems and stories. I wanted to be famous, or famous enough to be on television. Maybe, just maybe, I could be like Evelyn, and poetry could get me there.

What I did not consider was the high wire that Evelyn the Public Figure was gingerly walking across: the media's titillating coverage of her experience as a teenaged sex worker brought notoriety and people to her story, but her story was bigger than that. She was, in the most radical way possible, beating back at the respectability her parents and society wanted from her, the kind of respectability that had, for generations, seemed like the only path that Asian women could walk to survive the hierarchy of white supremacy. But the media only had enough space for one narrative, and they chose the less challenging one. People were only too happy to superimpose Evelyn's face onto every Asian female stereotype, ranging from the Nerdy Girl to the Sex Kitten. But, of course, Evelyn the Real Person had a brain and a body and feelings too.

I was consumed with the prospect of literary fame, with Evelyn the Successful Poet, the East Van girl who had fled the drudgery of damp corner stores and steamy noodle restaurants and liquidation centres. Perhaps they weren't racialized clichés, but still, I applied my own labels. I couldn't yet see beyond Evelyn the Public Figure either.

♥

I have tried to write this essay in a myriad of ways, to fold the fragments into a single narrative that flows from one shard to another, that imposes a structure on a topic that resists the light and instead slips in and out of shadows. It's not about my father's death, not about the multiple sexual assaults I have lived through, not about my divorce. It's about Asian fetish.

As a writer who has written about abuse and trauma for most of my career, I know that the most effective way to help people understand a concept, an ideology even, that marginalizes, oppresses, and dehumanizes a group of people is to say, "This is what has happened to me." It is this individual spectacle, in all its visceral, fleshy detail, that pierces the heart and brain and makes readers feel our pain as we have felt it, as we feel it again while we are remembering and writing about it. Abstract monologues get us only so far. Describing the smell of your boyfriend's hair, the striations of his muscles under your fingers, the weight of his body on yours just before he assaults you—this re-trauma accomplishes far more than simply saying, "He hurt me."

I resisted writing about my experiences with Asian fetish for many years, and I have been on the verge of trashing this essay over the years I've spent writing it because of how painful it is to put such intimacy on the page. But on March 16, 2021, a white man walked into three Atlanta-area massage businesses and murdered eight people, six of whom were East Asian women. Their names were Soon Chung Park, Hyun Jung Grant, Suncha Kim, Yong Ae Yue, Xiaojie Tan, Daoyou Feng. I say those names to myself as much as I can, to honour them but also to remind myself that writing about Asian fetish is, in fact, a necessary act.

When I first read of the hate crime, I was at home, writing as always. As soon as I saw the reports, I knew this moment was one I had feared all my life. Robert Aaron Long said he blamed these women for his sexual addiction, which is just another way of saying his fetish for Asian women was the motivating factor—a fetish that could only flourish because the racist assumptions he had made were wrong, damaging, inhumane, and, in this case, deadly. When there is an empty space where real representation could be, stereotypes—and fetish—fill that void. If you believe all Asian women are the same—all submissive and demure on the outside, sex-crazed on the inside—then you cannot believe we are fully human. Real humans get angry sometimes. Real humans don't always feel like fucking. Real humans, unlike fetishized stereotypes, are harder to murder. Robert Aaron Long wanted to have sex with Asian women, people he believed were subhuman in spite of his desire, and I assume he must have felt deep shame and self-loathing, his fetish and racism poisoning him from the inside out. But rather than punish himself, he chose to direct his anger at women who look like me.

In the days following, every major news outlet in Canada called me, asking me to appear on their shows to talk about the shooting and the environment that had led to it. I didn't cry until I was on the phone with a producer who asked, "How has this made you feel?" I burst into tears then, and I don't remember what I said in response, but I do remember the producer saying, "I'm sorry. I'm so sorry," over and over again.

I said no to all the media requests except for one, and I only agreed to the interview because the host is a dear friend of mine. If you heard it, I'm sure you heard the anger in my voice, the specific rage that occurs when the disaster you knew was coming finally arrives and only now do people listen.

I remember the host asking, "What can we do to stop this racist fetishization?" And I laughed with so much bitterness and said, "If I knew the answer, I would have ended it all a long time ago."

I have never shared where my own experiences with Asian fetish began, or how it felt when it was just me and a man alone in a room and I understood what was happening. I am trying now, with urgency, to write the words that can explain this to you, and to myself. Maybe it will work, maybe not. But I will approach it the best way I know how: by looking outward to the culture that helped me, in turn, look inward.

♥

In her 2001 collection of essays titled *Inside Out*, Evelyn Lau wrote, "The prostitution is what has remained."

Once, in a magazine profile about me, a journalist wrote, "Jen Sookfong Lee has a pretty face and knows, it seems, that sex sells."

The prostitution, you see, is what will always remain.

♥

I was twenty years old and cradling a telephone receiver under my chin. The raindrops, or, more accurately, rain-needles, were flinging themselves against my mother's kitchen windows. It was an angry storm, the kind that used to chill the house from the outside in until everything—the floorboards, the studs in the walls, the rattling pipes—shrank with the cold. In the early evening dark, I was listening to my boyfriend break up with me and I didn't have much to say.

I should probably clarify: he wasn't really my boyfriend. This boy—let's call him James—and I had been dating for a little over a month. We had met in an undergraduate class on the Canadian long poem, a very specific literature course that was usually only half-full, but whose few students were an oddball collection of poetry nerds, aspiring songwriters, and bearded philosophy majors who worked Derrida into every discussion. First, James introduced himself to me, shaking my hand formally with a lopsided grin as I tried to avoid looking directly into his sharp blue eyes. Then we met over home-work, reading and rereading lines of longing, place, and loss by Robin Blaser, Daphne Marlatt, and my favourite, Roy Kiyooka. He asked for help in choosing the right pair of shoes during the annual sale at the big Vancouver skate and snowboard shop, then he took me to a Sloan concert. We wore matching chains on our wallets. He wrote poems. I wrote poems. He told me mine were better. I knew he was right.

We had not talked about our relationship, made any commitments, or even seen each other more than a couple of times a week. But I had grown very attached to him. He played in a punk band, idolized T.S. Eliot, edited a literary journal, surfed in the summers and boarded in the winters, and was everything my post-grunge, rave-adjacent self thought she wanted. He said, "You're so cool. Why do you even hang out with me?" And my heart paused, as if it wanted to stop time and draw this moment out forever. After all, I had spent almost half my life curating myself so that one day, a boy might say this very thing.

That November evening, he told me he was getting back together with his ex-girlfriend, a girl he had met at his high school in the suburbs, a girl with a curvy ass, brown curls, and a complexion that I imagined people described as peaches-and-cream. When he was done explaining that this wasn't about me, that I was great and pretty and smart, I said into the heavy silence, "But why?"

"What do you mean *why*?"

"Why are you going back to her?"

He didn't pause at all. "Because she's comfortable."

I looked down at my narrow lap, at my hands with their short piano-playing nails, at the pink Chinese slippers with the plastic soles my mother always made me wear inside the house, and I knew exactly what he meant. She was like him and I was not.

♥

After James broke up with me, I saw him once with his new girlfriend at the year-end music festival that our university staged every April. That year, the festival featured 54-40, Mudgirl, and Pluto, exactly the sort of lineup both of us would be sure to buy tickets for. I had been drinking cheap beer for hours when I saw them, standing to the side of the crowd, his arms holding her from behind, as she swayed to the music.

She was tall and stood with her chin up, her body straight and confident, like she knew how to take up space and not apologize for it. Maybe she was a dancer, I thought. Maybe she never had to hem her jeans. If we stood next to each other, the sunlight would pool around her first—around her curly brown bob, around the smooth white skin of her clavicles. Six inches shorter, I knew only parts of me would be touched by the light, the rest obscured, lost in the dark. She would not notice. No one would.

I could not imagine taking that light for granted.

Feedback ripped through the air as the concert raged around me. I shrank into myself, pulled my corduroy jacket tight, and slipped back into the crush of people bouncing to the music. I was easily hidden. I'm sure they never even saw me.

♥

While James and I were together, I wrote a poem in which I compared him to a beam of light and described my body as small and cast in shadows.

listen he says
it takes time
do you understand
what does he see
that my mother is a heathen

and I am obsessed
with darkness
I blink.

In Evelyn's 1990 collection, *You Are Not Who You Claim*, she writes:

he watches you now with that cool reservation
only guilt can bring
on that slow painful descent down the back stairs
he puckers his lips
whistles at the sightless constellations.

These narrators long to be seen as they are, but they are not. They are obscured by the night, dim and dull compared to the brighter things. There is no one to see how much they can become, how they might transcend the invisible stairwells and burst forward, into the light.

♥

When I was just entering adolescence, two movies cut to the core of my emotional development: *Say Anything* and *Dead Poets Society*. Both movies, which I have seen over a dozen times, were released in 1989, the same year I first read *Runaway*.

To say I was in love with the young male actors in these films is an understatement. My dedication to all of them—and to John Cusack (who played Lloyd in *Say Anything*), and to Ethan Hawke and Josh Charles (who played Todd and Knox in *Dead Poets Society*), in particular—verged on obsession. At the time, all of them had unformed baby faces, their jaws hidden by the smooth lines of recent childhood. Cusack was tall and gangly, Charles was spotted with acne, while Hawke seemed to stumble over his own feet and have trouble speaking around the tongue in his mouth. Unlike the perfect faces of other teen actors like Mark-Paul Gosselaar and Johnny Depp, these three were not-quite-handsome outliers, boys with crooked teeth and close-set eyes, boys who were the very best versions of ordinary young men.

It wasn't just their looks but also what their characters embodied that compelled me. Lloyd, Todd, and Knox weren't alpha males, like John from *The Breakfast Club* or Blaine from *Pretty in Pink*. Lloyd play-boxed with his young nephew. Todd wrote poems that he then crumpled up in frustration, a pile of discarded paper on the floor of his room. Knox rode a rickety bicycle in the snow to catch a glimpse of the girl he loved. They were boys who held anxieties in their bodies, who didn't rage when things didn't go their way but cried or vomited or stammered through sentences that seemed to be still forming in their brains. The worlds they were living in didn't understand them and their little subversions—whether writing bad poems or smoking weed behind the neighbourhood convenience store. These gentle boys nursed broken hearts. They were lonely. They felt every last emotion.

I had grown up with a father who had been sick with cancer for almost my entire childhood before he died when I was twelve. Masculinity was a mystery to me. Until my sisters started dating, the only men who came into our family home were the ones who arrived via the television or books. Mr. Darcy. J.R. Ewing. John Ritter. My eldest sister obsessed over Harrison Ford. Penny, the sister closest to me in age, listened to Duran Duran all night long, even while she was asleep.

As for me, the page- and screen-based boys I grew to love were sometimes timid, usually creative, often painfully sensitive, and always, always white.

♥

There is a trope of the sensitive young white man who longs to be an artist or a cultural firebrand or a relentlessly free and idiosyncratic individual. In my favourite teen movies, characters like Lloyd, Todd, Knox, as well as Scott from *My Own Private Idaho* and Mark from *Pump Up the Volume*, try to be the young men their fathers and society want them to be—but then the cracks start to show. Scott has been groomed his entire life to take over his father's mayoral legacy, but he briefly escapes the weight of his family's expectations when he chooses to live on the streets. Mark is a friendless and awkward teenager, the boy who lurks by the lockers in glasses and Eddie Bauer plaid shirts, stuttering in response if someone speaks to him. At home, he starts his own pirate radio show, making masturbation jokes and speaking the heavy truth of early nineties teenhood into the night.

These boys are too queer or too liberal or too artistic to make a socially successful, academically productive adolescence possible. For them, high school is always a nightmare of social anxiety and rigid rules that they can never follow. But by the end of these movies, they have usually changed the system somehow, making their world and the people within it more ethical or kinder or more aware. In *Say*

Anything, Lloyd explains his future plans to Diane's money-obsessed father, starting an anticapitalist speech with "I don't want to sell anything, buy anything, or process anything as a career," proving himself to be the antithesis of status and wealth, things her father commits crimes to obtain. In *Dead Poets Society*, it's Todd who is the first to pay tribute to the disgraced Mr. Keating, who has been fired from his job as English teacher in the aftermath of a student's suicide. In *Pump Up the Volume*, Mark's truths about society and the pressures of suburban aspirations cause a high school storm, and as authorities close in on him to shut his radio station down, he broadcasts from his mom's old Jeep, his girlfriend at the wheel, shouting a revolution of realness into the air. They are saviours, emblems of goodness through subversion, if goodness could be accomplished through teenaged rebellion.

It's an attractive myth, one that satisfied both my emerging political and romantic selves, and ensured that a certain kind of girl would pay to see these movies over and over again. I was boy crazy. I wanted to fall in love, have a boyfriend who wrote me songs, told me his most painful secrets, and organized protests against clear-cut logging. One day, we would run away together, his skateboard tucked under his arm, my notebook of poems packed underneath thrift-store sweaters in my duffel bag. Instead of Ione Skye with the white orchid in her hair or Samantha Mathis with that brick-red lipstick against her pale skin, the girl in the movie would be me.

But the fact remains that the perfect, sensitive white man is a myth. These movies made these boys into heroes who conquer jealous ex-boyfriends, social expectations, and their own oddities, all the while maintaining their ethics of equality or socialism or creativity. In real life, of course, boys are not so easily deified. In real life, I already knew that they could be cruel, that the songs they wrote were often bad, that they, just like the sporty boys, fell in love with the most beautiful and popular girl at school, the girl who was most decidedly not me.

♥

Opening these old poems—Evelyn's from 1990, mine from 1996—is a brain-fuck. I read them with my head in both the past and the present. I try to read them as my younger self, a girl writing about love for the first time, a girl discovering that Evelyn writes about love too, but also about the lack of it, the imbalance of it, all the ways it can never be perfect.

"O in my dreams I resist premeditated applause," Evelyn writes. "I slide down rainswept streets where / fantasies clothe me splendidly enough." Expectations are never to be trusted. All we have are the stories we create. These are what will comfort us, love us back.

And this, from my twenty-year-old self:

you came this close
to wandering
into this space
and falling
this close
you are only human
but what am I.

The spaces between love and not-love seemed so narrow then. If I was lonely, was it a game of chance, or was I unlovable?

But the truth is I can never read these poems as I was in 1990 or 1996. My brain as it is today asserts itself. I am a mother now, a woman firmly in her midlife, and when I read these poems what I feel is sadness. I want to wrap these young women in a blanket and cook them lunch, show them they are enough with my hugs, my gifts of books and chocolate. They might never believe me. But I would try. I would try.

♥

After my divorce, I dated another man—we can call him Paul—whom I speedily fell in love with. He was Indo-Canadian, an extrovert by every conceivable measure, with a wide smile that seemed to precede the rest of his body whenever he walked into a room. He was not the first man of colour I had dated, but he was the first one I allowed myself to imagine a future with, even though there were fissures in our relationship from the very beginning. The most significant was how scarred I was from leaving a difficult and conflict-filled relationship with another man, someone I had met when I was trying to find my footing as a newly single mother. I still struggle to define that relationship to this day, how it had started with this man's effusive declarations of love, then ended with a dramatic fight in the middle of the night that left me spent and hollow for weeks. However, what bound Paul and me together was that we understood, at a core level, both the generationally and emotionally fraught relationships we each had with our families and cultures, and the very particular experience of

85

growing up in a traditional immigrant household and wanting desperately to escape it. This felt, well, comfortable.

On our first date, he told me how his father didn't speak to him for three years after he removed his turban and cut his hair. I told him how I hadn't talked to my mother in months because of her ongoing shame over my failed marriage. "Wait," he said. "You're thirty-nine years old with immigrant parents and this is the *first* time your mother has disowned you? Lucky you."

We dated through the spring, and by the beginning of summer, we had broken up but remained friends. He came to my book launches, sent me joke texts about the hip-hop music I love, chatted with me at parties like it was no big deal. Our commonalities, based on mutual respect and the push and pull of our cultures, were a solid base for what was becoming a supportive friendship. By the fall, he had a new girlfriend, a beautiful blonde woman with creative ambitions and peaches-and-cream skin, the kind of woman an Ethan Hawke character might fall in love with in a movie about a midlife man's second chance at love. If I were a man of colour who had watched romantic movies starring Julie Delpy and Vanessa Paradis and Scarlett Johansson my whole life, I would have fallen in love with her too. She was the woman everyone knows is pretty, the one the boys followed down the hall in tenth grade, the one who knows how to smile in photographs as if she is truly happy.

There were twenty-one years between James and Paul, and yet the breakups felt tied together. Yes, I had felt connected to them both in deeply fundamental ways. With James, I felt a connection of interests: we read the same books, liked the same music, made fun of the same frat boys on campus. With Paul, it was a connection of origins:

we had both defied our families, he by choosing to no longer wear a turban, me by leaving a secure fourteen-year marriage that everyone approved of.

They had both committed to white women shortly after dating me, a fact I tried not to think about. But I did. I thought about it a lot.

I thought about the times men would message me on OkCupid and ask if I was Chinese or Japanese or Korean. About the times my boyfriends would say they loved my smooth skin and narrow ass. About the white men who approached me on the street by saying *Nee how*. And about how I was a good time, not a long time. And then I felt a deep, deep shame.

♥

In *Say Anything*, the character of Diane, played by Ione Skye, is the picture-perfect pretty girl. She is good at school, devoted to her single father, and valedictorian. She is beautiful, but not the sort of beautiful that alienates. Her face is round, dotted with freckles, and she is socially awkward, uncertain of how to relate to or dress like the other eighteen-year-olds around her. She isn't a cheerleader or a cool-as-fuck bad girl. She is the sort of beautiful that bookish, awkward girls could be on their very best days, in the very best light.

When I was a teenager, I was good at school too. Like Diane, I was a school leader, the editor of the yearbook, and one of the founding members of the Gender Equity Club (we fundraised by selling T-shirts that shouted "Vaginal Pride"). Teachers loved me. The other kids respected me. Other girls would tell me their secrets. Boys asked me for dating advice. Unlike Diane, though, no one ever told me I was pretty.

I was also good at being social. Looking back, I see glimmers of the confident adult I would become. I was never afraid of speaking my mind, of being onstage to act or read my poems or deliver a speech. I had many friends, from every kind of high school clique you can think of—the popular girls with the perfect makeup, the boys who tried to breakdance in the hall, the writing club bookworms, the D&D nerds who haunted the photography and television studios. My life was busy, except for those weekend nights when my girlfriends were out with boys on dates, when I would stare at myself in the bathroom mirror and chart all the things wrong with my face that were preventing the perfect, sensitive boys from falling in love with me. My wide, flat nose. My undefined cheekbones. My short stubby eyelashes. The only thing missing, I thought, was beauty.

The summer I turned seventeen, I decided to make a change. I replaced my glasses with contact lenses, learned to apply eyeliner properly, and found clothes that actually fit my body. When I scrutinized my reflection in the bathroom mirror again, I thought, *I am pretty enough.*

That September, I was achingly ready to fall in love with the first sensitive boy who looked at me twice. He would love Jack Kerouac and Smashing Pumpkins and boozy peach cider. He might have blond hair or brown hair or hair that had been dyed in a pattern of polka dots. He might drive a 1983 Honda Civic with a hole in the footwell, so you could see the pavement rushing underneath you. He would read my poems and tell me they were good, that I should send them to a literary journal, perform at an open mic. I would listen to his demos, tell him he sounded just like Chris Cornell. It never occurred to me to question the race of the boy in my head. Because he looked the same as every actor and musician I idolized. Which is to say, he was white.

But I wasn't white or white-passing. And slowly, as the breakups accumulated, I came to understand that I didn't look like Ione Skye, that my family home smelled like star anise and Chinese soup, that I had never learned a winter sport, that my mother had never read a single word I had written. If these boys dated me, it wasn't because they recognized my life in their own. My parents never told me I could have any career I wanted. My family didn't own a cabin on a Gulf Island. I would never like camping. If these boys dated me, it was because of my difference.

I was skinny and Chinese and cute. I could speak Toisan and Cantonese. I could cook spicy noodles and watch a Wong Kar-Wai film without the subtitles. I was small. I avoided conflict. When a boyfriend cheated on me at a beach party, instead of confronting him, I walked away silently. I didn't know it yet, but I was a fetish.

♥

In *The Diary of Evelyn Lau*, the 1994 made-for-television movie based on *Runaway*, the character of Evelyn, as played by a young Sandra Oh in one of her earliest roles, is often hunched over, heavy bangs and giant glasses covering most of her face. She slips into alleys and huddles in doorways, covered in an oversized denim jacket as the neon lights of Vancouver ripple across her body. When she first begins to watch the other girls displayed under the street lamps in their short skirts and high heels, she looks afraid but curious, staring at them almost longingly.

Slowly, she transforms herself into what she thinks a sex worker is supposed to be. She wears the right revealing clothes, takes the right drugs, learns to speak the right words that the johns want to hear. Her roommate at a group home helps her with this transformation, pulling out clothes that reveal and perform. Later, once Evelyn is an experienced sex worker, she stands with confidence on the sidewalk until she spies her mother, walking alone. With a fragile bravado, she struts toward her and says, "Hello, Mother." But as soon as her mother's eyes travel over her skin-tight pants and blood-red lipstick, Evelyn deflates, her spine curling over once more.

How hard she had to work to be visible. How easy it was to disappear.

♥

In 1986, I was ten years old. That year, everything in my world seemed to explode in crackling technicolour like never before. My father was in a brief period of remission, able to garden and supervise my school field trips. The summer was warm and sunny, without any of the rainstorms that usually mark Vancouver well into July. I had a season's pass to Expo 86, the international fair that featured pavilions from participating countries, including my favourites Switzerland, for its giant Swatch watch that hung over the entry, and Hong Kong, where dancers in unitards performed in front of a film that slowly panned across the famed, sparkling Victoria Harbour. The soundtrack made me giggle as a choir sang with palpable earnestness, "Hong Kong, a city of pleasure, a city of joy!" I biked with my friends through the gravel alleys, my bare legs pumping up the hills, the blood rushing through my body. My father had been sick for so long, I had forgotten that feeling alive could be simple, could be experienced without guilt or foreboding or dread.

That same summer, Tamlyn Tomita burst into Hollywood, playing Daniel LaRusso's love interest, Kumiko, in *The Karate Kid Part II*, a franchise so wildly popular that kids around the world began wearing headbands and high-kicking their way through schoolyards. I didn't care for the martial arts, but I did care about Tamlyn, who was the very first Asian woman I ever saw in a mainstream American movie. She had everything: a wide smile, a dancer's posture, a perfectly symmetrical face. I saw the trailer on television and stared at her face, mesmerized by her smooth, graceful beauty, and by the possibility that I could be beautiful too one day, when I learned to control my cowlick, when my braces finally came off.

I sat down in a theatre with my older sister and her boyfriend, expectant, vibrating.

There is a pivotal scene leading to Daniel and Kumiko's first kiss, when she offers to serve him a traditional tea ceremony. You can Google it and see for yourself. Kumiko carefully unwraps her tools, whisks the matcha powder with hot water, folds and refolds a red napkin. She pours a cup for Daniel, but not one for herself. After he has finished drinking, she pulls a pair of chopsticks from her hair, releasing the long strands down her back, and then leans forward to kiss him gently, the camera pulling out until all we see are their two bodies—hers in a formal kimono—silhouetted against the window.

If you had asked me then why I hated this scene, I would have only said that I hated all kissing scenes and that tea is boring. If you ask me now, though, the answer is very, very different.

All the hallmarks of submission are there: the tea that is made for the white man but no one else, the closed-mouth smile she offers him from across the table, the quick hair transformation from prim beauty to unleashed object of desire. All of this pokes at the anger I feel about stereotypes, but there is one aspect above all else that speaks specifically to fetish, to the burning anger in my gut I have been feeling my entire life.

This scene is short, just a few minutes, and yet Kumiko manages to embody the two sides of Asian fetish with startling efficiency. She is coy and silent, willing to serve a white man's needs, but she is also subject to her own untameable desires. She loosens her own hair. She kisses him. She cannot contain herself.

The message is obvious: inside every well-behaved Asian woman, there is a sexual tigress waiting for her chance to pounce. At ten years old, this was not something I specifically considered, but even then this scene, with its symbols of tradition and submission, made me squirm in my seat. I wanted to ride my bike into the wind, write stories, and lie on a patio lounger to track the clouds across the blue sky. Serving tea to a man felt like it could be a punishment.

That fall, my father was back in the hospital, and he would never live at home with us again for longer than a few weeks at a time. That freedom, those moments of pure and rushing elation, were confined to that summer, and what remained, what trailed its way through the rest of my life, was the sinking feeling that I could never be exactly who I wanted or build my life around my own wants and needs. And that men, especially the ones who claimed to love you, were just another duty to tolerate, even if they hurt you.

♥

Asian fetish is difficult for me to explain in abstract terms, because its foundation is rooted in intimacy, those relationships between humans that are rarely seen by anyone other than the two people involved in that particular dynamic. The realization that someone is fetishizing you because of your race is a slow-dawning revelation. Often, you don't know it's happening until he rhapsodizes about the women who smilingly served him mochi and tea while he was teaching English in Japan, or he shows you his collection of manga featuring barely clothed female characters. Maybe he holds you and whispers that he loves how small you are, or talks about the qualities of your perky breasts. Maybe he frowns whenever a white woman expresses her opinion on television and then turns to you and says, "Asian women are so much more polite, so much more feminine." Maybe he tells you what he thinks about every topic under the sun but never asks for your thoughts in return.

I was almost forty before I understood any of this. In my twenties, there was the man who showed me his authentic samurai helmet and then lectured me about not knowing how to speak Mandarin. In my thirties, there was the man who said I should act in porn because I had the body every man wanted to fantasize about. Then there was the man who whispered, in bed, "I've always wanted to fuck a hot Asian girl." I accepted all of this. I didn't chastise them. I didn't tell them to leave my house and never call me again. The feminism I had learned from Gloria Steinem, Simone de Beauvoir, even Camille Paglia didn't cover this. No one ever told me what to do if a man treated my race like a sexual trophy. The artsy white man who took moody photographs, the biker-jacketed man who liked monotone independent rock, the woke single dad who dressed in fishnets to watch *The Rocky Horror Picture Show*—they all wanted to be with me, and for a time I thought maybe their desire would fill me with enough love and cultural validation that not even a disturbing race fetish would matter.

And this was what I felt the most shame about.

♥

Anna May Wong in *The Thief of Bagdad. Madama Butterfly*. Ming-Na Wen in ER. Gwen Stefani's silent but still cute Harajuku Girls. JinJoo Lee, the DNCE guitarist who never speaks.

All of these moments of representation are points on a timeline. Each generation has its own Asian female stereotype, a woman on whom whiteness can project its racist ideals. These clichés—of smallness and silence—have always bled into assumptions about sexuality. The submissiveness we see in mass media leads to a stereotype about submission during intimacy, about *doing what you're told* as an object of desire should, about the objectification that Asian women are supposed to enjoy but that actually leaves us vulnerable to aggression or abuse. These assumptions are so very old, marked by history and conflict, and they exhaust me, every single time I try to wrap my head around them.

Pornography, particularly online pornography, features Asian women and their capitalist value heavily, and this spotlight is directly related to the colonization of Asian women and their bodies. Colonization has touched many Asian countries, bringing with it soldiers who are far away from their families and wives.

Colonized women have never fared well, not then and not now. Their bodies become battlegrounds, currency, and R and R, all at the same time. The comfort women of Korea. The women trafficked across borders to work in massage parlours. The women raped as a tool of genocide. The women left pregnant by American soldiers during the Vietnam War.

In all of these examples, in porn and beyond, Asian women are tiny, with boyish bodies, and all of them suffer silently or near-silently, their stoicism reading as submission. Hypersexualization and presumed submission create a perfect storm of fetishization. Asian women are beasts in bed. Asian women will let you perform every sex act on their bodies that no one else will. Asian women don't complain when you don't text them back. Asian women have the tightest pussies.

♥

I remember the day when I started to push back against Asian fetish and its manifestations. I had been using dating apps off and on for two years, and I'd developed a policy that whenever anyone messaged me with even a whiff of fetish, I would ignore them. But the shame I felt at this silence, which was passive aggressive at best and complicit at worst, had been building. I had been ignoring the signs of fetishization my entire adult life, mentally weighing the pinpricks of racial sexualization against the characteristics I had always wanted in a partner. Does he laugh at my Jonathan Franzen jokes? Check. Does he own *The Pillow Book* on DVD? Shit. Does he only buy organic produce? Maybe he's all right then.

Then the year I turned forty, I received this message one evening from a man with a greying beard and a woollen cap: "You seem like a good, pretty Chinese girl." I wrote back, barely thinking, "Only two of those three things are true. You can guess which ones."

A few days later, another message, this one from a tall man with light eyes, written in Chinese. I wrote back in English, "Do you send this message to all the white women too?"

These replies were small acts of protest that may not have made an impact on the men who received them. But the replies weren't for them. They were for me, and for my younger self, who didn't know that being told I was small and sweet and smooth were really the expressions of fetish disguised as compliments. They were for my heart, cracked by James and later Paul, when they committed to women who were nothing like me. They were memorials for my earlier devotion to the fictional Lloyd Dobler, Knox Overstreet, and Todd Anderson, for the sensitive, creative, trembling white man who I was told was good and pure underneath his nervousness but who never really existed. They were for my future partner whom I hadn't met yet. They were for the shame that I hoped never to feel again.

♥

I still don't know if it's possible to write all the layers and nuances of Asian fetish accurately, or if it's hopelessly tangled up in complications I would rather leave alone. Being desired feels good. Being desired for my race, to the exclusion of every other quality that makes me an individual, feels demeaning and dehumanizing. There is a scene in *The Diary of Evelyn Lau* where Evelyn is recounting a conversation with a john: "He said I was good-looking. I thought he must have cataracts." The disbelief in her voice breaks my heart because this conversation is so familiar I can feel it deep in my bones. When I was eighteen, I met a U.S. Marine who, after two days, said he loved me, even though he barely knew me. My response was not to thank him but to say, "No, you don't. That's crazy." I knew, even then, that what he loved had little to do with me, the Jen who wanted to write books and drink fancy wine. Asian girls are never the ones the boys choose in the end, after all. In *Miss Saigon*, Kim shoots herself when she realizes that she will never form a family with her American soldier lover. In *Mean Girls*, two Asian female students—neither of whom ever speak a line of dialogue in English—are both sleeping with the high school football coach who sees them as disposable and interchangeable. In season two of *Friends*, Lauren Tom's character, Julie, is written off as soon as Ross realizes that Rachel is in love with him. After a month, that Marine stopped calling and I knew I had been right. He didn't love the real me. He loved a cliché.

Maybe when the john tells Evelyn she is good-looking during a brief moment of intimacy, he means it, but in the end, she is the sex worker and he is the man who will pay her and then go home to his wife. Evelyn, in this scene, understands the fetish but also longs to believe the compliment is real. I understood.

Separating the strands of race and fetish and desire has been one of the hardest things for me to learn or, rather, unlearn. Still, to this day, my insides turn to goo whenever I watch a movie with a stammering sensitive boy with clear blue eyes. *(500) Days of Summer*. *Notting Hill*. *Clueless*. What I tell myself is that this boy is no different from other men. They will forget a birthday, arrive at your house forty-five minutes late, come home from work tired and angry, and shout at you because you are the only one handy. They might watch too much porn. They might cum on your face without asking. They might ask you to pretend to be submissive while they whisper about your smallness, and those words will make you feel even smaller.

All of these topics are intertwined, tangled up in knots that I may never be able to untie. I fell in love with sensitive white boys on film. I looked for love. I accepted being treated as a fetish. I was dumped. And I loved hard, I really did.

I went back to *Say Anything* and *Dead Poets Society* after my marriage ended, trying to relive my love for these boys on film, seeking comfort during those long hours of night after my son had gone to bed. As I watched, I was lulled with the gold and green of a New England fall, the lines of boys in uniform walking to classes in limestone buildings. The charm of both movies was still there, in the shots of Todd and Knox running through the woods in feral joy, in the slacker lean of John Cusack's body.

But slowly I began to see that the young women who are the objects of the boys' affections are incidental, symbols of girlish perfection that are impossible to emulate. Who could be like Diane, so devoted to her father yet also beautiful and smart? In *Dead Poets Society*, there are the two pretty girls in pencil skirts who silently listen to the boys read their poems, and then there is the ethereal yet earthy Chris—blonde and dimpled—who becomes the object of Knox's romantic obsession without saying more than three lines to him. What real young woman could be such a perfect audience or a perfect object?

The writing teacher in me bristled—none of these girls go through any real character development. They are only there to passively respond to what is foisted upon them: lovestruck boys, fathers who disappoint, a looming adulthood they have not yet planned for. They inspire the boys to devotion. In turn, the boys pursue them with an unwavering obsession, refusing to accept rejection, returning to the girls' homes, trying to be indispensable in their lives by holding their hands and stroking their hair through fear and uncertainty. Knox reads Chris a poem in front of her classmates. In *Say Anything*'s most iconic scene, one that has been spoofed and replicated by comedians and copycats for decades, Lloyd stands in Diane's yard playing their song, "In Your Eyes" by Peter Gabriel, on a boombox he holds above his head. And my middle-aged brain thought, *Oh, Lloyd is actually a stalker.*

It was painfully clear to me that these boys were never more lovable than anyone else. As it turns out, these fictional boys played into the worst parts of obsession. Diane and Chris were girls who barely spoke before they became objects of desire. They were simply there, beautiful girls with good reputations, around whom each young man created a narrative of love and romance. Lloyd and Todd and Knox were never perfect. They might have read literature and railed against capitalism, but they were also driven by their own sexual egos to pursue these young women until they were worn down and acquiesced to relationships they had initially rejected. I could finally see: even these fictional boys objectified girls they barely knew. In my many years of idolization, I had believed that the sensitive, creative boys would never hurt anyone, would never hurt me by assuming I fit into a fetishized stereotype; as I watched Lloyd insist on making his presence known to Diane when it was no longer welcome, I knew I had been wrong my entire life.

♥

There is one more thing I haven't told you yet. And this is very hard for me to write about. Breathe in. Okay, here we go.

One evening just after midnight, during the aftermath of my separation, I came home from dinner with one of my closest friends. It was February and cold, and I ran up my front steps to get to my elderly dog, Molly, who would need a walk before settling in for the rest of the night. As I unlocked the door, I heard the murmur of the talk radio station that I left on to keep her company, playing through my wireless speakers. When I stepped in, Molly was agitated, running to me as she hadn't done in a few years. She licked my face nervously as I bent down to clip her leash to her collar and, in that moment, I realized what I heard in the background was not the station I always turned on whenever I left the house, but Peter Gabriel's "In Your Eyes." I stood still and silent, waiting for the song to end. When the song finished, it started again.

I knew then that someone had been here, the ex-boyfriend whose obsessive love for me had left symbolic scars that marked my relationship with Paul for failure from the very beginning. He had stood at my front door, signed into my wifi with an app on his phone, and programmed this song on a loop. "In Your Eyes," the song Lloyd plays for Diane under her bedroom window in *Say Anything*, after she has told him to never contact her again. I had told my ex about that scene, about the many ways that movie defined me. I had joked that there was no such thing as a romantic ideal, and this scene, riddled as it is with problematic issues of consent and obsession, might be as close as we could ever get. Laughing, I said I had been waiting most of my life for a man to stand outside my house and play this song from a boombox held high above his head.

We had dated for almost a year. For at least half that time, our relationship had felt out of control, wobbling on an insecure axis and throwing off the balance of everything else in my life. He had often been angry, focusing his resentment on things I couldn't always predict: my son's custody arrangement, my close relationship with my friends, an essay I wrote that did not mention him. He compared me to his high school crush, another Asian girl with a boyish body, and proudly showed me his shelf of books written by Asian women while I murmured approval I didn't feel. He dominated conversations with my male friends, pushing his way in until they stopped talking or until they pushed back, starting heated arguments that I inevitably had to diffuse. Our breakup, even though it was painful and emotional, was the first moment in our relationship where I felt like I could walk a straight line without wavering, no longer assaulted on all sides by the moods of a man who wanted to keep me and who wanted to belittle me as often as he could.

There I was, dizzy with the realization that he had come to my home and used the most significant film of my boy-crazy adolescence to mark his territory, to remind me that he could throw me into a tornado, if he wished. He had been a sensitive, creative white boy too, one who had cried when he told me the story of his parents' divorce, who had written lyrics from his favourite alt-country songs on a chalkboard hanging in his home, who had read all of my books before I ever met him. That night, I sat on the floor, Molly's furry flank pressed up against me, and I cried from fear and shame. Fear of him and the sensitive underdog exterior that masked his tightly wound rage. Shame because I had let him into my life at all, that I had been duped, that I was still mesmerized by a decades-old manufactured fantasy that had never been made for me in the first place.

♥

In the decades since I first saw Evelyn Lau on television, I have thought often about her fourteen-year-old self navigating a world she didn't yet understand, with its landmines of abuse, addiction, exploitation, and the desires of the thoughtless men who could simultaneously uplift and degrade you. I have thought about her poems, the words she furiously wrote in cheap notebooks, and how her emerging talent could not sustain her in the same way her body did at the time, providing her with money, places to stay, and even temporary love. Evelyn is now in her early fifties, an acclaimed, award-winning author who mentors emerging writers whenever she has the chance. I'm in my forties, an author, a mother, a respected member of my various communities. And yet the traces of my old life, and the boys who marked it, are still visible. Most days, I never think of them. Other days, when a white man follows me from the bus stop, or another stares at me for too long before whispering to his friend and laughing derisively, it all surfaces again. I am reminded that to some, I am Asian enough to fuck but not white enough to keep.

In 2017, I went to a party for a feminist literary festival, held at a former porn theatre in East Vancouver. There, in the lounge, I ran into Evelyn and another Chinese Canadian writer, Fiona Tinwei Lam. We talked about writing, about new books, about the fancy speciality cocktails at the bar. The room was filled with red-tinged light. After a few minutes, the conversation turned to how the publishing industry, and readers, view us, the handful of Chinese women who write books in Canada. I said, "If I had a dollar for every time someone called me Evelyn," and all three of us laughed. But the laughter was suffused with rage, with the knowledge that reading our books makes white readers feel better about themselves and their commitment to diversity, even if, most of the time, they still can't tell us apart. We are, in a way, objects in a game of literary fetish.

Fiona said, "Let's a take a picture. To prove we're not all the same person."

I stood in between them, and we smiled as the flash lit up the night.

Three hours later, I went home with a white man who unbuckled my shoes and held me as I slept, and I tried to believe it was love. He left at seven in the morning, and when I looked at my phone in the ensuing silence, I saw that photo of our three beautiful Chinese faces, the red light like a cloud of fire—or love—behind us.

THE
BAD GIRL

ONE: BE GOOD

I am eight years old. I am in my grade three classroom, working in a group with my best friend Lucia, who is also my greatest rival for grades, good behaviour awards, and adult attention. She wears two neat brown braids and a Benetton sweatshirt with leggings. I am in my usual navy-blue sweatsuit that my mother bought at Woolco, the discount department store on Kingsway.

Lucia points at my sheet of foolscap, where I have written the main duties of the prime minister. "That's wrong," she says. "See? The textbook doesn't say anything about parades."

"I saw him at a parade in Chinatown once. Besides, we're supposed to use our own words," I answer in a growl.

"No, it's just wrong."

She stares at me, challenge in her straight-backed posture and long-lashed eyes. She is so pretty, so sure of the right answer and how well-behaved she is. She is even a champion figure skater, a fact she repeats regularly. She and her parents live in a Mediterranean-style brick house, the kind with hanging baskets full of seasonal flowers and a matching sofa set in the living room. Her mother is a paralegal and drives Lucia to school every morning before heading to her downtown office in a skirt suit and pink lipstick. I have bed-head. My glasses are smudgy. My father has been hospitalized with the cancer that will kill him four years later. My mother stopped taking me to school long ago and I walk the three blocks alone, breaking into a sprint when I pass the yard with the snarling German shepherd who flings himself at the fence as soon as he smells me.

Lucia points at my worksheet again, a frown on her usually dimpled face. I scratch at my shin through my sweatpants, the same spot I have been picking at for weeks, and I can feel a scab break away. I have probably started bleeding again and this seems right, what I deserve. I look at the pencil in my hand, newly sharpened and shiny yellow, the only perfect thing about me.

With the sharp point of my perfect pencil, I stab her in the back of her hand. Her doe eyes well up with tears before she starts to scream.

Later, I am in the principal's office, staring at my shoes as he sits behind his desk, hands clasped in front of him.

"Jenny," he sighs, "you're a good girl. What happened?"

I don't remember if I ever answered him.

What I do remember is this: his star student was Lori Fung, the 1984 Olympic gold medallist who danced across the gymnastics floor with a big smile and long blue ribbons. Her photo hangs on the wall behind him, her body bent backward at an angle that seems impossible, one hand twirling the ribbons that spiral behind her. When I squint, I can see that her face looks a little like mine: a wide nose, tanned skin, long ears. But of course I am not the one with a gold medal future; I am in the school office for stabbing my friend with a pencil, wearing a sweatshirt dotted with toothpaste stains. I look back at the principal and Lori Fung stays suspended high on the wall, smiling through the most important—and flawless— moment of her life.

♥

When Amy Tan's first novel, *The Joy Luck Club*, was published in 1989, it was an immediate bestseller. A novel about four Chinese mothers in San Francisco and their American-born daughters, it was not an entirely unexpected success; Amy had sold it to her publisher for a then-astronomical fifty thousand dollars based on a few short stories and a proposal, an unlikely and lucrative beginning for a debut author. Very quickly, *The Joy Luck Club* became a phenomenon, the first mainstream book about Chinese Americans to truly become enmeshed in pop culture.

I read it in 1990, after my sisters had read and passed around a paperback copy among themselves, this literary sharing the closest the five of us came to a conversation about the realities of our lives as Chinese women. We were in the eye of the grief storm then, my father's death triggering a series of changes that saw my sisters propelling themselves quickly into an adulthood that had been on hold while he was sick. There were engagements, then weddings, then new apartments, and no time to process it all, much less talk to one another in any meaningful way. I was fourteen, still living at home, and cocooned in my bedroom as my mother was cocooned in hers. I read the book quickly, and then immediately started reading it again.

At that age, there was very little I had seen or read that burrowed into my Chinese girl heart. There was Evelyn Lau's *Runaway*. There was the brief cameo made by Sandra Wong in Margaret Laurence's novel *The Stone Angel*. And that was all. No actor on a daytime soap opera looked like me. No dancing girl in a music video. No protagonist in a young adult novel. Instead, I grafted my face onto the ones I saw and built my daydreams around a collage of other identities. Sometimes I felt like I belonged. Mostly, I didn't.

There is magic in representation, in that moment while reading a book or watching a movie when you come across a word or a food that you know in your bones, something you have known for as long as you have been alive. For people who have been marginalized because of race or gender or sexuality or ability, the first time they feel that shock of recognition, it reverberates throughout their bodies. They may spend the rest of their lives chasing it with very little payoff. Because, for most of us, representation is an exercise in scarcity, rarely abundance.

In *The Joy Luck Club*, there were Chinese mothers who could never understand their American daughters. And there were daughters who consciously chose not to understand their mothers, whose parenting, so built upon strictness and the fear of shame, was confounding. There were hidden histories, secret boyfriends, ambition, and disappointment. There were girls who binged ice cream and purged, and girls who stopped playing chess, even though they were prodigies. Girls who wanted love, but the show-offy, American-style love, the kind that smelled like freshly baked cookies and Chanel No. 5 (the perfume I always imagined white women of a certain age wore). Their mothers, trapped in homesickness, regret, and cultural isolation, didn't and couldn't give that love, and were left, in their old age, with daughters they no longer recognized.

I read *The Joy Luck Club* in my room, separated from my mother by a long hallway, in two days. The only time she spoke directly to me or my sisters during that time was the screaming match between her and Daisy, ostensibly about Daisy's upcoming wedding, but we all knew my mother was terrified of losing another person and didn't know how to say so. My mother, illiterate in English and barely literate in Chinese, couldn't read this book, but I wished, so hard, that she would. I didn't know if any book could help her say what she felt or recognize what we felt, but maybe this one could, if only she could read it.

♥

I am eleven. I walk up the front path to my piano teacher's house and stand at the door, as I have been doing every Saturday for a year. I hate my piano lessons, paid for by my mother so that the upright my parents bought for my sister Penny would not seem like such a waste of money. I had asked to learn the oboe, but my mother shook her head and said, "Girls should never put objects in their *mouths*."

I hate this house, where the windows are never open and I am pressed down by layers of cooking smells and shower steam. I make a decision: I turn around and walk back to the bus stop. I never come back.

♥

I have a confession. For a long time, I hated *The Joy Luck Club*.

There is something unremittingly *Chinese* about the stories in that novel, a classic example of the type of immigrant narrative that mainstream North American readers have always been eager to believe. Families come to the United States or Canada in search of a better life, escaping a culture that is restrictive both culturally and economically. When they arrive, the parents suppress their own professional dreams to support their households and become shop-keepers, dry cleaners, taxi drivers, restaurant owners. Their children are born, bespectacled and tiny, and grow up navigating two cultures, adhering to tradition at home and then shedding it at school, where they yearn for brand-name sneakers and a date with the most popular kid in class—Matt or Ashley or Danielle. Conflict arrives when adult decisions need to be made and secrets are revealed. It could be about wanting to go away to college or move out of the house, or choosing who to marry. And then, after a period of estrangement, during which life is simpler for everyone but also much, much emptier, a resolution, both emotional and narrative, is reached, often over dumplings and tea, or another elaborate meal that the mother of the family has loaded with symbolic ingredients. Longevity noodles. Long beans. Prosperous whole steamed fish.

The book's enormous success made *The Joy Luck Club* a modern template for the North American Chinese story, a template that every subsequent book by an immigrant or first-generation Chinese writer would be compared to. In the years following, the number of published Chinese American and Chinese Canadian female authors grew, but very slowly. In Canada, there was Sky Lee and Denise Chong and Larissa Lai, and in the United States, there was Sandra Tsing Loh and Shirley Geok-lin Lim, all of whom wrote extraordinary, ground-breaking novels that found solid readership, but none of their books ever reached the level of fame and ubiquity as Tan's. Time marched slowly for Asian women. Margaret Cho, whose Korean family sitcom *All-American Girl* aired for one season in 1994–95, and whose fame peaked dramatically (she even dated Quentin Tarantino) before fading out, knew better than anyone that Asian narratives had to fit into a certain box in order to succeed. "The weirdness of being the first Asian American—I guess, for lack of a better word—star, is that people are constantly judging you," she said in 2014 in an interview with *KoreAm*. "They're asking, 'Where do you fit on this idea of who we are?' With ethnic identity, there's a right way to be and a wrong way to be, and that's a really weird thing."

There was very little room for the funny, the raunchy, the silly. For better or worse, *The Joy Luck Club* was how non-Chinese people often learned about our culture, seizing upon well-worn tropes like the piano or chess prodigy, intergenerational cultural conflict, and familial ghosts. Like all clichés, these were rooted in truth, but the great diversity of Chinese narratives was lost when this book—slickly marketed, omnipresent in bookstores—became the only one remembered.

It was, in many ways, the version of Chinese-ness the English-speaking world was ready to accept.

♥

In 1993, when I was seventeen and my hair was dyed burgundy, when I longed to haunt underground raves, when I first read Elizabeth Smart and Sylvia Plath, the film version of *The Joy Luck Club* was released. I watched it in the theatres with my friends—Ellie, Ronni, the Other Ronni, Debra, and Julia, all Chinese girls like me, who had grown up in East Vancouver, whose parents had pushed us to be good and do better. Ellie would go on to medical school. Ronni became an engineer. Debra is now a human rights lawyer. Back then, we were just starting to apply to our undergraduate schools, fighting with our parents daily about what we were planning to study, where we were going at night, who we were dating.

By the time the movie was halfway done, my friends were all crying. I was not.

Every part of me hated this version of Asian womanhood that was unfolding before me. The quiet resentments. The unsaid subtext revealed in the flick of a pair of chopsticks. The rhythm of mah-jong tiles against a shiny lacquered table. The women, young and old, in tasteful turtlenecks and long bobs. And the secrets: so many fucking secrets.

At my house, there were no secrets, only the raw physical exposure of my mother's every visceral, painful, uncomfortable feeling. My mother wept in the daytime, barely ever spoke to me, and sometimes exploded in rage when she noticed my presence. And then there was me, in my thrift-store plaid pants and frosted lavender lipstick, writing poems about blow jobs and hand jobs and boys in fast cars. I hated turtlenecks. They made me itch.

When the final credits rolled, I sat curled in on myself, while my friends discussed what they had just watched and how they had felt seen. Four years had passed since the book was first published, years that coincided with my fast-changing adolescence. When I had read *The Joy Luck Club* at fourteen, it had felt as if Amy Tan had seen into the sadness and silence in my house and written a story just for me. But when I watched the movie, I was pushed away. Maybe it was because I was older, an almost-adult who had been looking for meaning in different kinds of culture, for a place that would nurture the writer in me, as well as the restless woman I was becoming. Maybe it was because the movie provided little room for me to insert myself. I wasn't Ming-Na Wen, with my hair brushed neatly behind my ears, peering sadly around a doorway as her aunties stacked the mah-jong tiles. I was just me, angrily stomping through life, wishing I could shake my mother out of her years-long depression, wishing my long-term crush Dave would finally notice me. Or maybe it was because I no longer cared about adhering to the acceptable Chinese immigrant narrative; I was starting to write stories that pushed at the limits of what good Chinese girls could do, stories where young women made decisions that were confounding or frustrating or damaging.

If I could have, I would have stood on my seat in that theatre and yelled, "I want to misbehave!" *The Joy Luck Club* was decorous and subdued. And I was furious.

♥

When I was thirty-one years old, I flew to New York City to launch the U.S. edition of my first novel. My first full day, I walked all the way across Manhattan, the adrenalin pushing my body forward. I had to see it all, eat it all, absorb this moment because I knew, even then, that it might never happen again.

For Canadian writers, launching a book in the States, in New York Fucking City, is success made tangible. As I stood in Times

Square, turning my head in every direction, watching the lights flash brightly in the daytime, I wondered if everyone could see the elation on my face. *I am here*, I wanted to shout, *I have made it.*

I had a launch party in a loft space, ate Korean fried chicken in a tiny restaurant accessible only by a flight of narrow dim stairs, drank martinis in the grand hotel bar, walked into shops that sold both artisan doughnuts and handmade clothing, and participated in an outdoor book festival.

"This is Jen," my American editor said as she introduced me at the event. "She wrote a novel. It's like *The Joy Luck Club*, but Canadian."

The first time she said this, I fell silent. *The End of East* had been out in Canada for a year by then, and no one had ever described it that way. It seemed too easy, too neatly defined to accurately describe what I had spent seven years, almost the entirety of my twenties, writing. But there was something else, deeper than the apparent dissimilarities between the two books, that my editor's words were poking at.

By the time I had started writing *The End of East* at the age of twenty-four, I had already spent years pushing against what I believed Asian women were allowed to write. I longed to be considered a young hipster of an author, the kind of twenty-something woman who wore a hoodie in her promotional photos, who flirted with more established writers, and who always managed to win the book prizes, even if she claimed she didn't care about such accolades. The poems I had been writing—often about loneliness, cold oceans, and the streets of East Vancouver—were constructed to build this identity, an identity that was decidedly in opposition to the Chinese girls who yearned for their mothers' approval in *The Joy Luck Club*. I did this consciously until it became habit, this reactionary writing style that was generated not from my own voice, but from a desire to push back at someone else's. These poems found sporadic publication for a while, but then the acceptances stopped coming. I needed to write something else. But I didn't know where to start.

I always say that *The End of East* was the result of a haunting, specifically a haunting by the ghost of my grandfather. I had been working at an office in Chinatown then, and I walked by his former barbershop every day. I often felt his spirit was following me, sometimes silently, sometimes whispering sentences that seemed disconnected, but were really fragments of his life story. Or so I believed. I began writing these fragments down, and they grew longer and longer as I wrote threads to tie them together. I spent days staring at archival photographs of Pender Street so I could describe the sidewalks as they were in 1918. Soon enough, my grandmother's voice began haunting me as well, and her story, along with the fictionalized story of my parents' marriage, grew in a document that ballooned to sixty thousand words. This was how my first novel was born—accidentally.

The End of East is about three generations of a Chinese family, fractured identity, and the silences that develop when families are kept apart by malicious immigration policies. There are mothers and daughters, fathers and sons, disappointments and unresolved resentments. The characters cook with woks, spend most of their lives trying to escape Chinatown, and struggle with the chasms between generations. It was, well, *very Chinese*.

There were times, especially while I was promoting it, that I hated *The End of East*. I had been running away from *The Joy Luck Club* spectre for most of my life, but here I was, the author of a book that could easily slip into that box, if someone chose to see it that way, even if it was also about sexuality, the contradictions of home, and everyone's deep desire to be touched and loved. I had written exactly the novel that I never intended to write; it was a novel that insisted on its own existence, and then became my alpha story.

My editor in New York was Chinese American, and our work together had always been fun and productive. As uncomfortable as I was with her thirty-second summary, I knew that she was simply trying to position the book in the way that she thought would be most effective for white readers. The people we were talking to at this festival were overwhelmingly white, as book audiences often are. If my editor had compared *The End of East* to, say, *The Woman Warrior* by Maxine Hong Kingston, there would have been blank stares. As famous as Kingston is in academic and Asian literature communities, *The Joy Luck Club* had been a fixture on the *New York Times* bestseller list for years, made into a Hollywood movie, and was the kind of book mothers give their daughters for Christmas. No other Asian writer could match Amy Tan's fame. No one has since.

"Oh," the booksellers and other editors exclaimed. "I loved *The Joy Luck Club*."

I wondered how many of Amy Tan's books were introduced in ways that made her feel small, forced into a shape that she had never intended. I wondered if I could express this thought out loud, but then I thought better of it. I smiled in response, gripping a copy of my own book in my hand.

♥

I am preparing for the biggest solo event of my still-new writing career—one hour onstage by myself, followed by a cocktail party honouring my first novel, hosted by a fledgling but enthusiastic writers' festival in a Canadian resort town. I receive an email. The event's advertising has gone live. I scan the words until my eyes land on one line: "Come in your best Oriental costume to win a door prize!" And then: "Join us afterward for the Shanghai Nights cocktail party, with Chinese-inspired drinks!" My head spins and I try to blink the rage away. But it rises instead, until my vision is blurred and hot tears burn their trails down my face. Later, the festival director tries to explain by saying, "It was meant as a tribute," and I shout in response, "This is appropriation," and I am still not sure she understands. It's too late to pull the ads, but she agrees to cancel the door prize and the theme for the cocktail party. Only one person arrives in costume, with a pair of chopsticks holding up her strawberry-blonde hair. She asks if she can take a photo with me. I refuse.

♥

After *The End of East*, I wrote another novel—admittedly, a very strange one—about a teenaged girl who discovers the true story of Mollie Fancher, a Victorian spiritualist who, among other things, claimed to have abstained from food for fourteen years. My protagonist, a suburban girl with red hair named Cat, develops an eating disorder herself after a love affair gone wrong with her much older choral teacher. The novel pinged between the contemporary Fraser Valley and turn of the twentieth-century Brooklyn. There was a disjointed diary, an overwrought spinster aunt, and a rotting ham hidden behind the drywall. I sent it to my publisher, confident in the literary experimentation I was exploring and still flush with the success of my first book, the kind of success that I had naively assumed happened to all debut authors.

They declined it. There was talk about capitalizing on my existing audience and writing a story that wouldn't alienate my readers. *Oh*, I thought, *this book is too weird and not Chinese enough*. I stared at the manuscript, immobilized by the creeping dread that I wasn't talented enough to push the boundaries of what novels should be. I was no Jeffrey Eugenides or Michael Chabon or Zadie Smith. I was just Jen, who had failed at piano lessons and was now failing at writing too. I was afraid. Deep in my gut, where I had hidden my writerly ambitions for so long, I was afraid I was losing my publishing momentum, losing a career that had only just begun.

My publisher told me to write something else. And so I did, a novel about a young Chinese boy who accidentally meets a burlesque dancer in a Chinatown alley in 1956.

That book was riddled with problems from the very beginning. The title was changed a dozen times, until at the last minute we decided on *The Better Mother*—a far cry from my original and favourite title, *Strip*. We argued about the cover design. I was told there was too much swearing and too much sex, that they wanted to position it as a "beach read but literary," that they were promoting it to lifestyle magazines, the kind that offered makeup tips and one-pot recipes.

Influenced by Tony Kushner's *Angels in America* and the otherworldly medical satire photographs of the late artist Theodore Wan, my novel was never going to be a beach read, but I kept my mouth shut. The fear told me, *Shush now, Jen, they are publishing it, that's all that matters. Maybe it will all be okay.*

It was published in the middle of summer, a dead zone for book releases, and if twenty-five people read it, I would be surprised. The fear ballooned and I never wanted to write again.

The next few years were some of the hardest of my writing life. Creating in the silence a failed book leaves behind is one of the loneliest things an author can do. I was acutely aware that many of my peers, people I had gone to school with or formed friendships through the industry, were publishing critically acclaimed, prize-winning books. I had written one moderately successful book and one dismally failed one, and I didn't know what to write next. I could write an immigrant family story again or a sequel to *The End of East*, as my publisher had seemed to suggest I should. Or I could forge ahead with the themes my brain had been reaching for my entire adult life—violence against women and girls, the sexualization of Asian female bodies, the hidden poverties that bubble up wherever you go in Vancouver.

The only good thing about failure is that, afterward, your decisions are yours alone. No one checks in on you. No one tells you not to write the story that might upset readers too much. No one cares and, in that space, either you start caring yourself, or you stop writing altogether.

♥

It's an old adage that artists should feel free to create whatever and however they choose. This is an ideal state, but it's not always a realistic one. In order for this to happen, artists have to be free of every other concern that life brings them. They have to have a reliable income. They need someone else to do their domestic work. They must be unconcerned about the reception of their work, the desires of the audience. They have to be impervious to the ways social media can criticize a creator, picking on everything from their weight to their headshots to their gender or racial identity. It is no coincidence that this artistic freedom is most often exploited by white men. White men who have wives to take care of the children. White men who have agents and managers to take care of the business. White men whose parents paid for their lengthy M.F.A. programs, leaving them debt-free. White men who can claim to be apolitical, because theirs are the only bodies that are never politicized.

For Asian female artists, this limitless space is a fantasy. Our families have already created the borders for our lives, before we were aware that we would create for a living. And the social constructs of not-family—work, romance, friendships—reinforce those borders. Either you are the good Chinese girl who does well in a practical academic program, works at a career in pharmacy or finance, then marries a polite Chinese man who earns an income that allows you to raise children, or you are the bad Chinese girl who writes in secret after everyone else has gone to bed, then works in a restaurant or a clothing store while revising draft after draft of a novel that might never be published, and doesn't earn enough money to support your aging parents. The choice is distinct. If you are someone like me who has only ever wanted to create, who never imagined doing anything else with her life, one option could be comfortable but also suffocating and unremarkable. The other might feel free until you can't pay your rent because your books only sell to a niche market, if they sell at all.

The choice is, really, no choice at all.

TWO: BE DIFFERENT

My mother and I are watching the Miss Chinese Vancouver Pageant on television. The young women look stunned as they move across the stage in their gowns and swimsuits, answering questions in broken Cantonese but better English. The woman who wins is a childhood friend of mine, who used to wander the school hallways looking lost, her head turned down so she wouldn't have to make eye contact with other students. She dropped out three months before graduation. She has not had contact with anyone I know in years, and I had no idea what became of her until this moment, as last year's Miss Chinese Vancouver is pinning a tiara to her head. I think I see in her eyes a trace of her younger, more ghostly self, the one who seemed afraid of anyone who might speak to her. But her wide, winning smile soon takes over and she looks like every other beauty queen I have ever seen.

My mother sighs. "You could have won that. But you never listen to me."

♥

When I was thirteen, I started high school at an alternative academic program, one designed to fit the eccentricities of its students, many of whom had trouble with the structure of a regular high school and who showed promise in the arts and social justice. It was a tiny school, with one hundred students spread out over five grades. We painted our lockers every September. We held school meetings about our participation in peace marches and logging protests. We had a school dog named Charlie, a golden retriever who sometimes had seizures and loved Costco muffins. At this school, I learned to write freely. I performed improv. I learned about activism and how change occurs. These were all tremendous and rare gifts for a teenaged girl still trying to figure out how to express her grief over her father's recent death.

But I was also the only Chinese Canadian student. My friend Ronni, also a Chinese girl from East Vancouver, had initially attended with me but then transferred to a bigger high school, where her restless social spirit felt more at home. I stayed, because I was the creative one, and because, except for the race thing, it was the right school for me.

A group of boys, all white, began to call me Hello Kitty, a reference to the fictional feline character popular in Asian toys, anime, and accessories. Whenever I walked past them in the hall, they would shout, "Gotta get that A, Hello Kitty." They pretended to push imaginary glasses up their noses whenever I spoke up in class as my own heavy glasses slid further and further down my face from nervous sweat. They asked me why Chinese people cut down all the trees or built stucco mansions or sold all the drugs, mimicking 1990s Vancouver news coverage, which was heavily centred on wealthy immigrants from Hong Kong or Taiwan and on Asian youth gangs. These were stupid, racist questions, but these boys had probably heard their parents say similar or worse things at the dinner table. One boy only flirted with girls of colour but then used racial slurs to describe them when they weren't in the room. They asked me for math help. And I gave it. At that school, I wrote stories and poems that made me believe I could be a real writer, but then another student would ask me why people from Hong Kong always butt into lineups, and my soul would shrink. Either I was the good girl, the Hello Kitty with the straight As, or I was something more sinister, the kind of Chinese person everyone else hated for their fast cars, McMansions, and inability to wait patiently in line for an ATM. Except I was neither.

The next year, I followed Ronni to the bigger school, where there were more courses to choose from and a more rigorous academic program. And also there was a much bigger Asian student population. No one asked me dumb questions because the answers were already so very obvious. No one made fun of my good grades because everyone's parents expected the same. No one asked for math help because I was no longer the best at math. Far from it, actually.

And more importantly, there were so many Chinese girls there. There was the girl who dated a wannabe gangster and carved his name into her arm with a razor. There was the math prodigy who only showed up to class once a week, usually high. There were the identical twins who held court over the social hierarchy, like double Regina Georges. Among so many other Chinese girls, I could choose who I wanted to be because everyone else did the same. I didn't have to be Hello Kitty or anything else. I could just be.

I bought a star-printed batik dress, dyed my hair pink, wore silver-painted Doc Martens. I became the girl who co-founded the Gender Equity Club and wrote a poem for the classmate who died by suicide. I had a loud, emotional fight with the school's star actor, who I briefly dated. In front of 1,800 gawking teenagers in the cafeteria, he wailed, "I said I was sorry! What else do you want?" I escaped to the darkroom when it got to be too much and printed my photographs—all moody, all images of dilapidated garages and alleys in East Vancouver—until

I grew lightheaded from the chemical smell. I still got the As, and I was still a good girl, but I was pushing, ever so slightly, toward something that might one day fit me perfectly, if only I didn't get too scared.

♥

Google "Amy Tan sings Blondie." You will find a shaky video of Amy Tan wearing sunglasses, an enormous blonde wig, a black leather minidress, and fishnet stockings, as she half sings, half shouts "One Way or Another." In the background are other authors, all men, all white, playing guitar, bass, keyboard, and drums, dressed in nondescript jeans and T-shirts, but even they don't seem to notice their own existence. Everyone watches Amy.

This is the Rock Bottom Remainders, a band of famous authors (including arguably the most famous author in the world, Stephen King) that plays once a year for charity. They stick to rock classics like "Louie Louie" and "Bye Bye Love," but "One Way or Another" is Amy's song.

In this 2010 video, she is already fifty-eight years old. She dances and sings with sky-high confidence. She wags her finger at the audience, tilts her hips forward, never acknowledging the band of men behind her. Behind her sunglasses, she could be anybody. But she isn't. She is Amy Fucking Tan.

♥

In 2012, I started writing *The Conjoined*, the story of the Cheng sisters, two teenaged foster girls from Vancouver's Downtown Eastside who go missing in the 1980s, and the lone social worker who, almost thirty years later, tries to find out what happened to them. The novel was my love letter to the great contemporary crime writers who stare down the bleak and the difficult. Jo Nesbo, Ian Rankin, Elizabeth George, Gillian Flynn. The writing was challenging, leading me to develop passages of abuse and violence from the inside out, from the intimate—and painful—perspectives of both victims and predators. I leaned hard into the underbelly of Vancouver, where lives are interrupted and forcibly ended all the time, where sex and drugs are intertwined, where people try to get out but are often thwarted at every turn. I wrote about how the systems in place—childcare, immigration, social assistance, criminal justice, capitalism—defeat almost everyone who can't read and fill out the right forms, who are stuck at home with small children, who have the wrong accent or the wrong clothes, who get fired again and again. There are scenes of assault, death, and grief. I wrote about trauma and its aftermath, the ways in which we redeem ourselves.

This was not the book a good Chinese girl was expected to write.

It was the best, most exhilarating writing process of my career. I wrote in solitude. I wrote through my son's toddlerhood and a separation, and that novel miraculously held me together. All of that pain, all of that seedy, dirtbag Vancouver mess I was immersing myself in became a shield. When I was a child, my mother would take me shopping with her in Chinatown, which is part of the larger Downtown Eastside, then called Skid Row, and I was never fazed, never aware that this neighbourhood was extraordinary or different.

For many years, the Downtown Eastside has been called the poorest postal code in Canada, and it has always been a place where people with addictions and mental health issues live and congregate, partly because of the cheap single-room hotels, partly because it was where they found each other and the community they needed. People have always slept in the streets there, sold and bought their drugs, fallen in love, and raised their children. But it's the human misery that always makes the news, often triggering national headlines about overdose deaths and crime. It's not uncommon for my friends from other cities to ask if I can take them to the corner of Main and Hastings, so they can see the poverty with their own eyes. I always refuse.

Chinatown occupies the southeast corner of the Downtown Eastside, and both places have existed in tandem for as long as I can remember, sometimes peacefully, sometimes not. This was where my family first lived in Canada. It was where we returned to buy groceries from the streetside markets, checked in on elderly relatives who lived above the clan association, held wedding receptions. This familiarity, this mundanity was what I was writing. It was equal parts homey and dangerous. It was a place that could both nurture and destroy you. But it was there, as it still is, existing independently of every other neighbourhood in Vancouver, quietly breathing its life in a space that everyone else had abandoned.

I wrote these streets and their stories joyfully, something I wasn't even aware was possible. I have always had a deep, underdog type of love for the parts of my city that do not attract Instagram travel influencers, that are invisible from the penthouses in the surrounding condo high-rises, that contain the homes and lives of working-class Chinese families who are no one's model minority. I was honouring these spaces in *The Conjoined*, and it felt like the book I had been inching toward since the day I knew I wanted to be a writer. When the very foundation of my life was crumbling beneath my feet, I opened my laptop, began to type, and was happy. I had found my story.

♥

I did not know that Amy Tan sang in a rock band and dressed as a BDSM queen until 2013, when she published her novel *The Valley of Amazement* and I saw her appearance on a late-night talk show. In the performance clip they aired, Amy, wearing a black leather jumpsuit and hat, shouts into the audience, "You've heard of *50 Shades of Grey*? Well, this is *100 Shades of Tan*!" Of that moment, she says to the host, "I'm freed to be another person." Not the respected author of an international bestseller. Not the midlife Chinese woman with the tax lawyer husband. But a dominatrix sing-shouting into a bar, backed by a band of men.

In the middle of writing the novel that would change the way I saw Chinese Canadian identity, this clip of Amy Tan stomping her high-heeled patent-leather boots seemed to reach the very core of what I was writing about. There is more to our stories than what the world has been led to believe. There is subtext and laughter and kink. There are love stories and petty grievances. There is always, always more.

If Amy were sitting in front of me right now, I would ask, "Was this always you, deep inside where no one—not your family, not your readers, not your colleagues—could see?" I would tell her that I was always someone else inside, that this someone was unruly and restless, horny and mean, a night owl who believed beauty was most visible in the dim. "Maybe we are the same," I might say, if I thought she would be into that, if I thought I could see a familiar demon in her eyes.

I would ask, "Did you feel forced to be the good Chinese author, to be the woman who could speak to white readers and their assumptions, the publishing industry and its marketing plans? Did it ever make you want to scream or run away?"

Then I would tell her that I wrote a poem once about the inner self, the one that grows in the dark places until there is no more space and she bursts outward, into the surface of life.

Your old self never died. Untended,
she grew, unfurling sideways
under your uneventful, grownup life.
Funny how that happens.

The older I got, the more I needed to honour her.

Maybe Amy Tan is doing the very same thing, shouting her core outward, backed by a band, into a dancing, cheering crowd.

♥

I am on my first real date after my divorce, with a man who is wearing a sportscoat with elbow patches, because he knows I am a writer and he wants to look smart. He is magazine handsome, with perfectly styled silver hair and hipster glasses. When I first see him, I half turn my body, poised for flight. It would be safer, wouldn't it, to run away because if I stay, we will fuck. I will be unleashed.

I went back to his apartment many times. No one ever saw me coming or going.

THREE: JUST BE

"Everybody knows the secret now:
that when a woman sleeps with a man right away,
it's not because we don't respect ourselves.
It's because we don't respect you."

ALI WONG, *HARD KNOCK WIFE*

When Ali Wong's Netflix comedy special *Baby Cobra* began streaming in May 2016, she was relatively unknown outside of stand-up circles. Even I, a relentless consumer of all things pop culture and Asian, hadn't heard of her. With her big glasses and loudly patterned dresses, she looked more like me than any other famous Asian woman I had ever seen. My friends would say, "Have you watched *Baby Cobra* yet? She is just like you." I shrugged. I was used to being compared to other Asian women in the media, even if we were nothing alike. Newscasters, singers, the doctor who dispensed advice on her own cable television show. Sure, sure, they were all just like me.

But then I streamed it one night while I lay in bed, my son asleep in the adjoining room. Wong made jokes about her sexual past, about the condition of her pussy, about insulting Korean people when she and her husband are alone. Was the bearded man she slept with in her single days homeless or just a hipster? Is an HPV infection a badge of honour? Is it true that opinionated Asian women who wear big glasses only sleep with white men? (Spoiler: yes.)

I laughed. Hard.

Visual representation is one thing, a very important thing. But so is a representation of sensibility, of the thoughts you mull over but never speak, of the desires you've kept hidden, of the jokes you've only made with your closest friends over wine, in the safety of your kitchen.

We had seen so much Asian female pain. Ali Wong brought us Asian female joy.

Here was the joy and raunchiness of my innermost self being spoken by a woman I'd never met but who made me feel like I was looking in a mirror. Alone in my room, I laughed until I cried, my dog snoring on her bed beside me. Watching Ali Wong say what I had only kept inside made me realize I too could want things, I could be angry, I could be funny, I could be dirty. Readers seeking stories of subdued intergenerational conflict might hate that. Book prize juries looking for trauma narratives focused on the pain of immigration might hate that too. My mother for sure would hate that. But fuck them. Fuck them all.

The Conjoined was published that September. In every city I visited while on tour, young Asian women came to my events, most just barely in their twenties, and told me how they had connected with *The End of East* when they were teenagers and had followed my writing ever since. *The Conjoined*, they said, showed them what was possible, how Asian women could write characters full of contradiction and mess, how there was space for them in an industry that is still overwhelmingly white. A few cried when they met me. Almost all took selfies with their arms around me. And then I cried too.

I had written the riskiest, messiest, most visceral book of my life. And even after the writing was done, it was living a joyful existence. Imagine that.

♥

Recently, I watched *The Joy Luck Club* for the first time in twenty-six years. I procrastinated until 10 p.m., putting off what felt like an onerous research task. I had no real desire to be immersed in the sad Chinese lady world again, not when it was much more fun to watch Amy Tan on talk shows or Ali Wong's Netflix movie, *Always Be My Maybe*. When I finally pressed play, I heard Ming-Na Wen's voice drifting through the speakers, recounting a story about a swan feather. She sounded calm, mature, maybe even a little mystical. I snorted out loud. "Of course," I said. "Chinese ladies tell pretty Chinese stories."

But then the movie continued, a layering of mother-daughter relationships, each one distinct in its traumas and misunderstandings, though the trope was consistent: the mothers try to connect, but the daughters resist. The conflicts are about culture and language, American individuation versus Chinese collective reasoning. Success is never enough. Tough love is never enough. There is a vast gulf between them, and yet each pair of women makes their way toward each other, across emotional and also physical distances. I cried when Kieu Chinh's Suyuan left her twin babies by the side of the road, exhausted and injured from fleeing on foot from Japanese occupation during World War Two. I laughed at Tsai Chin's salty portrayal of Lindo, who schemes her way out of an arranged marriage and later tries to mould her daughter into a chess champion. I cried again when Rosalind Chao's Rose yells at her estranged, waspy husband, a very well-cast hangdog Andrew McCarthy, about how he never really tried to understand her true self. I cried. A lot.

Plus, the babies—and there are many in this movie—are impossibly cute.

I was falling under *The Joy Luck Club* spell.

The book and movie adaptation have both been called melodramas, with death and assault and war and madness inserted like ticking time bombs throughout. We know that bad things have happened to these women, that the past was painful, but when the trauma is finally revealed, we cry not with surprise but with recognition. These moments—of domestic violence, stolen children, dead bodies, loss, so much loss—are what Amy Tan and the film's director, Wayne Wang, prepare us for. Silence. A hard, yuppie version of Tamlyn Tomita stomping through houses in her corporate shoes. Lauren Tom sadly pouring tea in a grey angled house. All of these visual cues point to old hurts, the ways in which women are injured, abused, left behind. All of these point to a truth that I had been wrestling with for most of my life, ever since my father first fell sick: old trauma never really goes away. We might build our lives to accommodate its presence or ignore it altogether, but it can still be seen—sometimes faintly, sometimes obviously—no matter what. The respectable armour we wear can only hide the scars—of war, of racism, of generational conflict, of loss—for so long.

I had been wrong all these years. Maybe *The Joy Luck Club* was just another honest version of Chinese-ness. Maybe the cottage industry around that book, and the ways in which Amy was presented to readers and booksellers who weren't yet ready to examine their assumptions, created a larger mythology than any one author could have written. Maybe marketing and media pushed the easy, unchallenging versions of Amy's novel and identity. Maybe she was confined to a box too, one that I recognized but had wrongly attributed to her, Amy the real person. Maybe my love for this novel and for jokes about pussy could co-exist. There is truth in clichés and in dirty jokes. Neither would exist without it.

♥

Whenever I'm confused, I turn to Google. I look up everything that is driving my anxious brain. Sometimes it's the details of a vacation. Sometimes it's the Facebook profiles of my exes. Sometimes it's the private lives of famous people, because I need to believe that they are different than their public personae.

In the wake of *Baby Cobra*, I began searching for anything I could find about Ali Wong's off-camera life. Who was she when she wasn't telling off-colour jokes on a stage? What did she look like without makeup and those animal-print dresses? Was her then-husband as hot as she jokes?

Her Instagram page features posts about her comedy specials, her movies, her books—all the things you would expect. But it also includes videos of her dancing with her two young daughters, badly lit photographs of noodle soup and trays of dumplings, and her mother in an ugly Christmas sweater. Most importantly, it shows Ali herself makeup free, with her hair in a messy topknot, wearing giant stretchy pants in varying colours of mud. It's not funny, because it really isn't. It's just life, and a pretty respectable one at that.

Even though Ali Wong's Instagram page is highly curated, as everyone's is, it appears that she, for lack of a less overused phrase, is living her best life, one in which her work, her family, and every dumpling she can find are her priorities. This is what good Asian girls should do. The only difference is her work is based on jokes about vaginas and micro-penises, predatory men and foul-mouthed women. There is no explanation for her contradictions, for the misshapen, messy ball that is her life. Ali is many things. She just is. Fuck, that's refreshing.

♥

While I was rewatching *The Joy Luck Club*, it occurred to me that Amy Tan is old enough to be my mother, that she is, in fact, a generation removed from me and my peers. Her version of Chinese-ness was never going to match mine exactly, but it was close, and it held some deep truths about mothers and daughters, duty and independence, home and away. This is what I couldn't see at seventeen, stuck as I was in a full-blown teenaged rebellion. Amy Tan's words—so careful, so considered—were something I felt I had to push back against. She was my literary mother and I was her ungrateful, shady daughter. Amy couldn't have written it better herself.

In the middle of the movie, Tamlyn Tomita's Waverly picks up a roll of foil-wrapped condoms and hurls them into the air, where they unravel and fall to the floor of her beautiful San Francisco home. Her mother, Lindo, simply sits there. "Aren't you going to say something?" Waverly shouts.

"What do you want me to say?" Lindo says quietly. "You want to live like a mess, what should I say about that?"

Waverly's face falls because her tantrum, which might have felt good to her in the moment, has had no effect. No matter how bad she tried to be, she wasn't really all that bad, was she?

The truth is this: I am still a good girl. For the most part, I think about other people's feelings, I parent with intention, I write and edit books that I think could make a difference in the literary landscape and also in the world. Maybe I drink too much on the weekends, and maybe I treated some men with indifference in the aftermath of my divorce. Maybe I am a little self-involved. Maybe I blame everything on my mother. But I am still good, with a hint of restless, raunchy, indulgent. I write literary books, but they're also pretty dirty.

When Ali Wong yells about her nipples and then goes home to her small children, when Amy Tan dresses in leather, sings badly into a mic, and then sits down the next day and writes a classically beautiful sentence, the truth of who they are is in the transitions. They are who they are when they need to be. In the transitions, they are all things.

You see, there are no boxes, no small spaces for us to contort ourselves into, not really. Those were created by others, makeshift prisons that we believed were for own good, because that's what they wanted us to believe. But those were lies.

What is real, and what I know for certain, is that there are spaces in which we move from destination to destination, spaces through which we move with so much velocity that we are impossible to define, spaces that require change, that ask us to access one of the multiple identities we carry at any given moment, that allow us to be as fluid as we want to be. It's a beautiful fact. And it's ours.

Tomorrow, I will go for drinks with my girlfriends and shout at pretty boys in a crowded bar. Tonight, I will make chicken rice, cuddle my dog and son, plan a holiday. In the transition, after I have dropped off my son with his father and before I brush makeup on my face in careful layers, I am a middle-aged woman in comfortable cotton underpants, waiting for the moment when the wine is poured and the music turns loud and I will be whoever I want in the shifting, pulsing light.

THE
RIHANNA FANTASY

THAT VERY BAD BREAKUP

If Rihanna were the boss of your life, this is how it would have gone.

Once you knew he was coming over, you would have listened to her album *Anti* ahead of time, especially "Desperado." Rihanna's clipped voice skims over the lyrics, words written, you think, for a lovesick man with an unpredictable gun, someone who is constantly on the run, both from the law and from the woman he believes is too good for him. "We could be runaways," she sings, "running from any sight of love." The song is about escape, about that moment when a woman considers leaving her entire life for a lover who sleeps in cars and bathes in rivers too muddy to drink from. Quietly, Rihanna sings, "There ain't nothing here for me anymore." Her old life holds no more appeal. And neither does yours, not anymore.

The song evokes flat plain highways, gas stations littered with tumbleweeds, a way out of the city that is both exhilarating and terrifying. There could be rattlesnakes, other men hiding in abandoned barns, dangers lurking everywhere. But this song would still be exactly what you need. Rihanna herself, through this song, would tell you what to do and you would listen until that moment you hear his heavy steps outside your front door.

This is what she would have told you: *We aren't afraid of him.* You agree, of course you agree. Everyone agrees with Rihanna.

You would have said, "I think we should break up," and he would have protested a little, a decorous amount, and you would have repeated, calmly, "We are breaking up. There's nothing here for us anymore." And because you faked a commanding presence, he would have left, closing the door silently behind him. You imagine him driving away in the night, on a flat plain highway. He unfollows you on Instagram, and it is done, it is done.

You play *Anti* again and again all through the night, and Rihanna's voice is the equivalent of a bartender setting down free fingers of whisky for your heartbreak, but also for your preservation of dignity. *Anti* is your reward for protecting your pride, for not letting an ex-boyfriend fuck with you.

You did this to yourself, asshole, you whisper into your glass, which you pretend is his retreating back.

But the truth is shameful and you hate it. The truth is that you didn't listen to Rihanna, not at all.

That night, what really happens is that you cup your nipples in your hands to dull the shooting pain and you remember the old photographs of Rihanna's bruised face, swollen in the unflattering police light. She was twenty-one then, and dating Chris Brown, that brash, confident singer whom all the girls dreamed of while listening to his bedroom songs. After he beat her in his luxury car, Rihanna might have said, *Never again.*

You whisper the same thing to yourself when your ex finally propels himself down the stairs and out the door. You are curled in a ball on your own bed, repulsed by his smell on your sheets, because he begged you to sleep with him one more time and it was easier to allow it, even if you wished you could abandon your body, your slutty, embarrassing body that is still capable of sex when sex is the last thing you want. *Never again*, you promise yourself. He calls and calls, but you keep your word, and this is the only real decision you have made that Rihanna would be proud of, but even then it's too late. The disappointment is yours and you imagine it's hers too, not that this makes your memories less malignant, less barbed. You don't listen to *Anti* again for the rest of that year.

WORKING OUT

If Rihanna were the boss of your life, this is how you would exercise.

You would dance to a playlist her assistant made, although Rihanna herself gave final approval because no detail is too insignificant for her attention. It would stream through hidden speakers in a room with mirrors lining the walls, a room at a secret address that you have travelled to, that Rihanna insists has the best acoustics, the best give in the hardwood dance floor. You arrive and the door is unlocked, but there is no one else there, just the sound of your soft-soled Pumas in the empty hallway. This workout time is yours and yours alone. You watch yourself in the mirror because Rihanna wants you to believe that your body is good and beautiful. It carries you through meetings and literary events, and through a crowd of mothers who you are pretty sure you dislike when you pick your son up from school.

You hear her voice. "Now *you* dance, Gorgeous."

You look at yourself with pride. Rihanna knows self-love is key and has organized the perfect ring light to illuminate your shiny hair. Your legs are good. That don't-fuck-with-me face is tight and you pump your fists in the air.

But there is no secret dance studio, no playlist that isn't suggested by Spotify.

No, what you really do is wait until your son is asleep or at school, close the blinds, and search for a YouTube workout video that takes no more than twenty minutes. You follow it as closely as you can, and you always mix up your left arm with your right, you stumble with the simplest quad stretch. There is no point in looking in the mirror because your body has never really been a part of you; it has been something to tolerate, to escape whenever possible.

You were a skinny child who could fold up your body and hide it away in the smallest, most invisible spaces you could find so you could read and write and play with your favourite Playmobil characters. Under the dining room table, with its long lace cloth. Behind the sofa, in the corner by the sliding glass patio door. Beside the rubber plant, under the leaves that grew toward the sunshine. You counted dust motes, fell asleep on the seventies-era orange carpet. No one could find you, not even your mother, who paced the house in angry circles, looking for the most convenient target. You were happiest when you disappeared.

When Rihanna dances, she touches her own body and you always stop to watch, mesmerized. In the video for "Wild Thoughts," she wears a teal transparent dress and caresses herself while the beat rises and falls. You believe she loves doing this, loves being present in her physical self, where brain and muscle and flesh are not separate entities but part of the same organism. You imagine she sings and laughs and drinks red wine with her whole being, feels the warm burn rippling through her head and belly and toes, as if her body isn't her mortal enemy.

What does your body make you think of? Sweaters and denim, the bulk and layers like a shield to protect the smaller you who lives inside, who is still afraid her mother will derisively point out that flat chest, the one buck tooth, the slouch in that noodly spine.

What does your skin feel like under your own hands? You don't know. Sometimes, when you are reading, you hear a noise, and you look up and see your reflection in the window and you startle at the stranger staring back at you. You never think she is pretty, and if someone else says you are, you never believe it.

Your brain always wants to be elsewhere, always wants to find another city in another book, but your body—your boring, mediocre, extraneous body—stays put. This surprises and then disappoints you, every time.

When you are done working out, the relief washes rushes through you. It is over. You have fulfilled your obligation to the body you have never loved, that omnipresent taskmaster, that always hovering parent.

THE FAMILY MEETING

If Rihanna were the boss of your life, this is how the family meeting would have unfolded.

You would have allowed your sisters to speak first because Rihanna believes in leading with benevolence. They outline their concerns about your mother's health, her finances, and then their feelings. This is fine. You have practised performing empathy your entire life. After all, you are the youngest in a big and sprawling family in which every sister, every brother-in-law, every aunty tells you their problems. At first, it was because you were small and had nowhere else to go. Later, it's because you have a good resting-empathy face— no smile, but thoughtful eyes, a wrinkle in your forehead that signifies concentration, even if you are thinking of a boy who just dumped you or the boots you want to buy.

Maybe you write disconnected words on the notepad in front of you. It's okay. You have an idea for a poem and, if you forget it, that's time wasted. Rihanna would want you to make every pocket of time productive.

You are the last to speak. They know to always give you as much time as you want. Up front, you ask for silence until you are done because you have boundaries, you know what you do and don't need. Everyone complies. Even though you're the youngest, they know better than to push at your limits.

You say:

"I am getting divorced."

"I don't want to be the family clown anymore."

"I have no capacity for betrayal."

Everyone agrees that your marriage has been dying for years and your terms are reasonable and fine. You smile, wide and bright. You pour tequila shots, the glasses lined up in a row, the bottle held six inches above the rims because you have more bartending confidence than you have skill. *Candy*, you say, *let's get candy*. You find a store that will deliver on DoorDash, and you fill your virtual cart with old-fashioned sweets: Cracker Jack, Super Lemon, Popeye Candy Sticks. And it appears twenty minutes later. Perhaps the delivery driver listens to Rihanna too.

Later, at midnight, your eldest sister will send you a drunk text, thanking you for your generosity, and you think, *Generosity is called something else when the giver demands reciprocity*. You feel no guilt though. Your sisters are tipsy and high on sugar. You will remind them of their promises, and your gifts, in the years to come. This pleases you.

The last thing you would do is hide in the bathroom, crying as you text anyone who might answer you while your sisters knock on the door, saying, "Please don't react like this. We are just worried about you." No, you would never run out of the house as they are still asking questions—*How hard did you try? Why would you want to ruin your child's life? Who will even date you?*—and walk three kilometres to your best friend's parents' house. She is staying there with her newborn twins, her breasts permanently attached to a pump, and yet you know she will make time to hear your complaints, to pass you a tissue from the box she keeps beside the nursing chair. And you would definitely not give up asking for what you need—help to keep your house, childcare support, some kind words, just one kind word—even if your family says no, eyes hard as they scan your face for any trace of emotion. You would never keep your feelings hidden, breath skipping against the hard balls of sadness in your throat. Except this is exactly what you do.

When you leave your next family party, you pull over in your car share and rest your head against the steering wheel in a wealthy neighbourhood, your exhaust pipe spitting clouds of smoke in front of a faux Edwardian mansion. There are no tears because you don't deserve self-pity. You were never strong enough to mourn a loss of strength. It's just you, crumpling under the weight of your family's gaze, like always. So what?

You turn on the car radio but it's not Rihanna, not "Umbrella" or "Cheers" or "Good Girl Gone Bad." It's Taylor Swift, and you roll down the window and let the rain pelt your face with sharp, angry pinpricks. It hurts, as it should, because you know what Rihanna would have chosen for you and you did the opposite. Such insubordination deserves no better than pain.

But as Taylor sings, you can hear her telling you to shake it off, and you bristle at the idea that it is possible to blithely move forward as if nothing hurts. Rihanna knows better. She knows that you have to ride out the pain, look at your scars, and never repeat a misstep. You think of her testifying at Chris Brown's trial in a pantsuit, her face still and resolute. Maybe she wept beforehand, but in the end she walked into that courtroom and told a judge how Brown had hurt her. You change the station and you find Imagine Dragons, a bad song with an epic, dominating beat, and this is what you need to remember to roll up the window, dry your face with your sleeves, and steer your tinny car share toward your cluttered little home. You promise yourself that you will play "Pon de Replay" as soon as you step inside.

THE
COUGAR

It was a hot July afternoon, and I was drinking rosé, as I did every Wednesday in my friend Miriam's kitchen. We had met when our sons were still babies, and we bonded as the boys grew older. When the school year was over, we'd set our children loose in her large grassy yard, open cold bottles of wine, and talk about our dying marriages. During those stretches of time, those long hours and days that were our only reprieve from rage and grief and loneliness, we both drank a little too much, complained just enough, and cried when we had to, when our wry jokes were no longer funny and our emotions erupted into the warm humid air.

Miriam lived in a heritage house, the tallest and oldest in our neighbourhood, with an impressive turret and a yard that spanned a quarter of an acre, a true unicorn in Vancouver. The house was over a hundred years old and required regular, extensive maintenance. That summer, the exterior was being painted by a company that exclusively hired postsecondary students. The painters became a fixture, as decisions had to be made about vintage colours, the intricate trim, and rotting soffits, and all of that took time, much more than Miriam had anticipated. The crew played hip-hop music, wore their T-shirts with the sleeves rolled up, and moved through their work with ease. When I walked past them, they appeared so young and beautiful and unscarred, an idealized version of youth, the loss of which I had recently been mourning every time I looked in the mirror in the unforgiving morning light.

That summer was the first since my ex-husband had moved out. I had met my ex when I was twenty-one, and now that my marriage was over, I was thirty-eight. Those seventeen years had sped past me. We bought a house, we got a dog, we went to Europe, we had a baby, we bought a bigger fancier house we couldn't afford. Every single one of these milestones was relentlessly *adult*, and if there had been a guidebook listing all the tasks you must complete in order to be a true grown-up, my life would have been its star example. But that summer, newly separated and on the cusp of forty, I was all too aware of how my face and body bore the marks of this adulthood in the stretch marks on my belly, the lines around my mouth, the white hairs I painted with mascara whenever I went out. That summer, I watched those flawless creatures, their bodies fluid in the heat, and tried to remember when I had ever moved with such smooth perfection.

Through the kitchen window, I watched one painter (we can call him Matt) standing on a ladder, working on the trim. He had taken off his shirt in the thirty-degree weather. From where I was sitting, I had a perfect view (what a cougar-y thing to say). He was handsome in that way that is enmeshed in Canadian culture—tall, broad-shouldered, with a sly, lopsided smile and sleepy eyes. Later, I would find out he had played elite junior hockey and was from a small town, where his father had been the school principal before being elected mayor. Matt moved like he owned every space he was in, taking his time as he unfolded a stepladder, stretching in the sunlight when he felt the need, never rushing to get a job done. He was exactly the kind of boy I used to admire from a distance at university beer gardens fifteen years earlier, the boy a friend of a friend might have dated, the boy I had never let myself have a crush on because he was too confident, too expansive with ease. It would have seemed futile to even bother imagining us together. When I was younger, I was the opposite. I buzzed with nervous energy, worried there was never enough time to read all the books, write all the books, and kiss all the sensitive boys who slouched through life in Kurt Cobain–inspired cardigans. I would never be fast enough or smart enough or pretty enough to get it all done.

Matt waved at me through the glass. I waved back. Miriam watched our exchange and then whispered, "I think he likes you," which made me laugh. *How ridiculous. What a concept.*

At the end of his workday, Matt came to the back steps to talk. I told him I was a writer and he said he was planning on attending law school. Miriam smirked and added, "Her ex is a lawyer. And she just got rid of him." Matt smiled his crooked grin at me and said, "Well, are you looking for a replacement then?" And I thought, *How old is he? Maybe he does like me? Why does he like me?*

I had yet to date anyone in my post-separation fog. I had been focused on selling my house and finding a new one, attending therapy sessions every week, and keeping up with my writing. Improbably, I was in the middle of editing a novel with a new publisher and serving on a literary prize jury, for which I needed to read over two hundred books. Dating was an amorphous concept, something I pushed to the back of my brain for later, when I had the time, when I felt better about the sun damage on my face and the stretch marks on my belly. It wasn't supposed to be now. But now, something was happening.

♥

I remember the exact day I started hating Gwyneth Paltrow. It was 2002, and I had just paid eight dollars to watch her film *Possession*, based on the Booker Prize–winning novel by A.S. Byatt. I loved *Possession* and had read it multiple times, the spine of my copy so cracked that the pages hung loosely, as if exhausted from all the late nights I spent flipping between chapters to read the carefully crafted lines over and over again. The plot centred on two modern-day academics—both stalled in their careers and romantic lives—who discover a clandestine correspondence between two Victorian poets, a record of an affair that had remained secret for a century and which now threatens to upend the scholarly world's understanding of their mysterious love poems. As the two academics pore over these fading relics of a long-dead romance, they fall in love with each other, their relationship a parallel to that of the poets'. *Possession* was everything I wanted to accomplish as a writer. It was a novel about love, postmodernism, and the polyglot ways we cobble together identities. I wanted to be brave enough to write a novel that was just as epic, that centred sweeping romance on a foundation of poetry, that left readers breathless at the end, when they realize that the two love affairs are unexpectedly tangled up together. I wanted to satisfy readers. I wanted to turn them on. And I wanted them to love my book as much as I loved *Possession*.

The film's failures were apparent to me as I sat in that theatre. *Possession*, in book form, is dense with footnotes, long narrative poems, and a shifting, sometimes hazy timeline. The film adaptation could only skim the surface of its source material, never really getting to its core critiques of class and fandom, its interrogation of the fallibility of literary biography and the costs of hidden queer love. The novel elicits emotions: we're angry that poets remain poor across time, and we despair for the lovers who can never declare their presence, who are then left behind, heartbroken. Perhaps it's impossible to adapt a book that is so layered into a mainstream Hollywood film. But for me, it was just a reason to hate Gwyneth. The movie sucked. It must have been her fault.

I was unreasonably, blindingly jealous that Gwyneth, the daughter of Hollywood legends, the once-girlfriend of Brad Pitt, the tall blonde rich girl who had never even gone to university was starring in this movie, *my* movie. It was an absurd hatred; after all, she had no idea who I was and likely wouldn't care about my feelings even if she knew about them. But my resentment wasn't about reciprocity. She was my celebrity nemesis and I was in her shadow, invisible to the world while she only shone brighter and brighter.

Gwyneth first burst into the celebrity ecosystem in the mid-1990s, when she appeared in prestige films like *Se7en* and *Sliding Doors*. At the time, I had shrugged at her WASPy, ice-blonde persona, which evoked such Hollywood Golden Age legends as Grace Kelly and Tippi Hedren. In the era of Lollapalooza and the Viper Room, Gwyneth's brand felt outdated and quaint, and I paid very little attention. But then she became the go-to blonde actress for literary films like *Sylvia* (a very bad biopic about Sylvia Plath), *Emma*, *Great Expectations*, and most famously, *Shakespeare in Love*, for which she won an Oscar for Best Actress. When she married Chris Martin, the lead singer of the British band Coldplay, best known for their sweetly written, alt-pop anthems, it seemed right.

She was cool enough to marry a rock star, but only the most genteel and inoffensive of rock stars, the kind who would never trash a hotel room but might wear designer leather pants. She moved to London. She gave birth to two blonde children who, the internet tells me, are already gifted musicians.

It didn't matter if I was the bookish one, reading in the dark. Women like Gwyneth had always had a glowing head start and were always going to win the imaginary war in my head.

♥

The only single parent I had really known while I was growing up was my own mother. Single motherhood had not been a choice for her; she was forty-nine when my father died—young for a widow—and her decade-long grief was at least partly triggered by the unfairness of it all. My life as a single parent began after I made the decision to leave a marriage that others had seen as contented and stable. At the time, I was the first among my friends to end a marriage, which meant no one could tell me which lawyer to call, what top to wear to the bar, or what to tell my son when he asked the inevitable questions about our disrupted family.

For as long as I can remember, I've been obsessed with popular culture—watching it, dissecting it, trying to pick up bits and pieces I could learn from or use in my own life. The post-separation me was no different, and was, perhaps, even more invested in how celebrities were performing their breakups. Kate Hudson, Scarlett Johansson, Gwyneth Paltrow—in the years after my separation, they were all newly single, and I was hopeful they might show me how this new life was supposed to work, that there might be some solidarity and solace to be found in the space between their public decisions and my private ones. I clicked on their paparazzi photos on the gossip sites, zooming in to see if they too were wearing sweatpants and slippers outside, if they looked exhausted, or sad, or just blankly numb, the way I did every single day. They were running errands in luxury denim and heels, or attending glamorous events in sparkly designer dresses, their children nowhere in sight, while I wondered what combination of shapewear, squats, and lighting would ever make me look like that. I combed through interviews they and other famous single mothers had done. I read every gossip blog to see who they were dating. Because of course they were dating. Of course they didn't have to wait for someone to see their desirability. Of course they looked better than ever.

Divorce gave them a new narrative that centred on self-empowerment and freedom, on their careers and personal lives taking flight beyond what their marriages could give them. Kate launched a line of very tight workout clothes. The message? Single moms should practise self-care! Single moms can have lithe bodies too! Scarlett delivered an acclaimed performance in *Marriage Story*, a movie about a crumbling relationship that capitalized on her own famous breakup and custody battle. The message? Single moms can turn their traumas into profitable art, even if they're too tired to brush their teeth at night!

And then there was Gwyneth.

When Gwyneth and Chris announced their separation in 2014, they famously popularized the term "conscious uncoupling," igniting a social media rage. It was clear that Gwyneth—and maybe Chris too—believed that she could perform divorce better than everyone else by simply resolving to do so. But what I already knew is that a friendly divorce and co-parenting relationship can only happen when everyone has all the money and support they need, when there is no overwhelming resentment or power imbalance, when paying for therapy is a matter of course. If you don't have these lucky circumstances, divorce can be an ugly process.

Then there was the way Gwyneth's separation was announced—not through a publicist, as is common for celebrities, but on the website for her lifestyle brand, Goop. One can imagine the conversation that might have occurred during the staff meeting that morning: Why not drop a huge gossip bomb through our growing business and drive some traffic to our retail endeavours? Why should Gwyneth fall apart after a divorce like everyone else when she can monetize the gossip and the clicks?

After her divorce, the Goop brand grew quickly. The Goop site, which launched in 2008, is where she sells and recommends a range of luxury products, including, most infamously, egg-shaped pieces of jade meant to encourage vaginal health. It takes only two minutes of browsing to see that her favourite thing to do post-workout is put on a pair of seven-hundred-dollar compression boots. Tickets to In Goop Health, a one-day wellness summit, cost one thousand dollars per person. What Gwyneth and Goop present is a completely different version of humanity, one that some might argue is barely human at all.

♥

When my son had his first panic attack, I knew exactly what I was witnessing. He was eight when they started, the same age I had been when my panic attacks began. And just as I had, he was reacting to the changes in our family. I held him as he kicked and screamed, and I cried. I had failed him. I had not protected him from our genetics, from the monsters of worry that loom and threaten when big changes are too much for small children to bear. I had failed.

None of them—not Scarlett, not Kate, not Gwyneth—could show me what to do. Their children were fine, or at least they were in public. Their co-parenting was flawless and safe and loving. As my son wept, I thought, *Fuck them, fuck them all and their perfection*. They had failed me and I had failed him.

My younger self had always been able to find role models in the culture around me when my real life failed to provide them. It didn't even matter when the players in that culture had very little in common with me; I was well used to grafting identities and behaviours. This time though, I could find nothing. My pop culture coping mechanism wasn't working. I began to hate myself.

♥

In a *New York Times Magazine* profile, journalist Taffy Brodesser-Akner describes visiting Gwyneth at her home in Los Angeles: a house manager named Jeffrey pours the wine, her ex-husband gives the children music lessons, and her current husband cuddles her while she cooks. Like many people who hate the very idea of Gwyneth, I combed that article for any sign that her life isn't the perfect and perfectly happy one she has been profiting from for years.

Not a spoiler: there is none.

Taffy herself appears throughout the article, spilling clam juice on her shirt, sneaking cigarettes to calm her nerves, taking phone calls about her panicked child back home in New Jersey. As she stares at Gwyneth's perfect size-eight arches, she's reminded that her own feet are broad and flat. Afterward, alone in her hotel, Taffy writes, "I thought about the word 'aspiration,' how to aspire seems so noble, but how aspiration is always infused with a kind of suffering, and I smoked another cigarette." Taffy, in this narrative, is all of us.

There is an enormous gulf between Gwyneth's life and ours, one that is very clearly created by wealth and privilege, something she seemingly doesn't quite understand or doesn't care to. "My life is good because I am not passive about it," she has said. Her life isn't good because she was born with almost every single advantage you can imagine. Her life is good because she is a go-getter.

And yet, despite all her assertions that her idealized capitalist happiness is wholly built upon hard work and positivity, she must know, deep down, that women around the world are unhappy, maybe even pathologically so. How do I know she knows this? Because it is precisely this unhappiness that she is exploiting for profit. Women with privilege like she has—generational wealth, a lifetime of tradi-tional beauty, an identity that is cis and white and straight—don't need Goop at all. They already know how to curate their own skincare or BDSM kit. They already know which restaurant to go to for the best ceviche. These are not the kind of women who turn to Goop for sexual health vitamins, lipstick shades, and party planning tips. No, it's the newly divorced mom who is staring down her fiftieth birthday and despairing over the elasticity of her vagina. It's the young woman who picks at her acne in the mirror and is afraid of losing her boyfriend when he goes off to law school. It's the woman who goes to work in a male-dominated company every day and wishes she could beat the men at their own game. Gwyneth is selling what these regular women are missing: a life of ease and beauty and, yes, privilege.

I could have been any of these women. Only instead of buying into what Gwyneth was selling, I directed hate and rage at what she represented, as many women do. If you google Gwyneth's name, you will very quickly see just how much vitriol she inspires.

When Taffy Brodesser-Akner asked Gwyneth why everyone hates her, she responded, "Because I have discipline?" There is no regret in that statement, no irony; it is presented like something we should already know. She appears to be blind to her immense privilege and to believe firmly in the myth of meritocracy; whatever is hers, whatever she has accomplished, it is all because she is more disciplined than the rest of us. If we could all wake up at five in the morning to the California song sparrow trilling in our private lemon grove, pass on our parenting responsibilities to the nanny from a developing country we can't remember the name of, and work out for an hour with our tiny and bubbly trainer before drinking a smoothie with acai, chia, flax, and other improbable ingredients, then maybe we too would have a closet full of neutral minimalist cashmere, a new husband who poses shirtless on our Instagram feeds, and a multimillion-dollar business in which we simply tell others what absurdly expensive items to buy.

As I struggled to keep my house clean, walk the dog, get my son to school on time, and wash my fucking hair, I hated her with an intensity that burned three times hotter than in the moment

Possession's end credits rolled years earlier. How can someone hate a person they have never met? I knew. Every time I saw her photo in a magazine or online, I knew. She owned and sold everything I didn't know I wanted but could never have. And the lack of it all, apparent in the small disorganized life I was living, fuelled my rage.

Even though I didn't buy any Goop products, I still chased after anything that promised glimmers of perfection that made me happy for a day, maybe two. My coping mechanism? I cycled through men I might not have liked all that much, just to try to like myself a little more.

♥

The first night Matt came over, I was entirely on my own, which was a rarity. My son was with his father, and I was alone in the house I was trying to sell. In those days, my friends visited often, worried about my depression, about how I wasn't eating enough and was drinking too much. They were beside me as I packed up the remnants of my married life. In those boxes were the dishes and tools and sheets I had used during my marriage, that I still needed to use, that they said I would still use a year, two years, or five years from now. It was all so bulky, so cumbersome. They helped me consolidate my past, my present, and my future, even when I desperately wished I could let it all go, let the weight pass through my hands like a long thread I never wanted in the first place.

That night, Matt brought me a bottle of bad wine and I remember he smelled like soap. Not like cologne or body wash or hair pomade, but good, clean, old-fashioned soap. Before he kissed me, he asked for my consent. He held me gently and I thought, *His mother raised a good boy.*

He said he thought I was twenty-five. He said I was pretty. He said he wanted to read my books. Maybe it was all a lie, but for that one evening, I forgot that my son was wracked with anxiety, that my clothes hung loosely on my too-thin shoulders, that every month I looked at my bank balance and cried with shame. Drinking wine with a handsome younger man meant I could pretend that I had never hurt anyone, that I had never failed my child, and that I could trick someone else into believing I was perfect enough too.

♥

The need to aspire, to become something better than we already are, is a direct symptom of capitalism, which sounds terribly heavy, because it is. But it's also a pretty simple truth. A capitalist society thrives on individuals feeling as if they are never enough and can never have enough. Countless products promise to fix that lack, and we imbue the products we buy with power because we are desperate to fill that yawning emptiness. What we forget, in the adrenaline rush of buying more stuff, is that the hunger can never be satisfied. It's a long, toxic con, with capitalism promising happiness in a shopping cart, but then upping the ante so that just when we think we are done, another product or path to happiness appears, leaving us to continue grabbing at what we can, whether we can afford it or not.

Idolizing beautiful Hollywood actresses for their seeming perfection is not new. Whole fanbases formed around Mary Pickford and Debbie Reynolds, actresses who were both perky and sparkly with girl-next-door wholesomeness. Companies took note and Mary Pickford appeared in print ads for everything from laundry soap to night cream. Debbie Reynolds, with her smooth bouffant, sold shampoo.

The difference between then and now is accessibility. In the last decade, social media, and particularly Instagram, has provided actresses with a way to speak directly to the fans who love them. If Mary Pickford had critical thoughts about her three husbands, or the quality of her night cream, no one ever heard them publicly. If Debbie Reynolds wanted to prove she was living her best life post-divorce, there was nowhere for her to share a radiant sunset selfie that also illuminated her shiny, shampooed hair. Now we can see photos of the tastefully fun decor at a celebrity child's birthday party, or the beach at an actress's exclusive vacation resort in Bali. And when we lift our eyes from our phones, we see our own lives— small homes we can barely afford, Lego stuck in the vacuum, produce rotting in the refrigerator because it was so much easier to order pizza after a long day. Our lives can never be good enough, not like that.

But maybe they could be, if we just ordered the same balloon bouquets or booked a week at the same resort. Our access to celebrity lives means they have access to us too, or, more specifically, to our purchasing power. Today's actresses are no longer just the smiling face in a magazine ad for a product they didn't make. Today, they build the companies that bring us those products. Today, they speak to us on Instagram Live, on YouTube, and in Twitter posts with embedded links. They are wholly, visibly in charge of how they monetize their fame.

The resulting dissatisfaction we feel with our own lives can be crushing. It can lead us to force starvation on our bodies, to chase after the next car or the next handbag. It can lead us to judge others for not having the right anti-aging serum or hair removal guru or healing crystal. It divides people, mostly women, into those who have the time and resources to buy, exfoliate, and meditate, and those who don't.

It led to me lying in my bed in the dark, furiously swiping on profile after profile on a dating app, looking for my next date. Or, more precisely, my next high in a life that was almost entirely made up of debt, emotional lows, and a messiness that Gwyneth would like us to believe she has too much discipline to understand.

♥

The next two years were a blur. I sold my old home and bought a small townhouse, where I moved after a flurry of packing parties. I found new jobs, wrote new books, lost my beloved dog Molly. My son's anxiety began to ebb away as we worked on his fears, the ways in which his brain always circled back to disaster whenever anything bad happened. I made new friends and lost some old ones.

The problem was that I still hated myself. And it was becoming worse every day.

When you choose to leave a marriage, the prevailing cliché is that you're choosing yourself, that you're practising self-love, that the marriage is a barrier that has been preventing you from achieving self-actualization. But what if you choose to leave a marriage because you are afraid of poisoning your family? Because you are afraid that your unwieldy anxiety and depression will one day snow your husband under? Because you are afraid that you will become your mother, hiding in your bed when you can't face another moment of plain everyday life, leaving your husband to pick up the unfinished tasks you have abandoned in your fog of sadness? That is the opposite of self-love, isn't it? It's a desperate attempt to pre-emptively save everyone else the pain of your dysfunction, to stop a seemingly inevitable catastrophe from happening.

Do you know what happens when this is your only choice? When you are finally alone and faced with the darkest parts of yourself that you wish you could light a match to and burn away? You see how ugly you really are, and you hate it. You hate yourself with an intensity that leaves you breathless and reaching for a distraction, any distraction.

If Gwyneth or Scarlett or Kate ever felt this way, they have never said so. It's easier to sell a post-divorce brand if the separation is rooted in self-care. Self-loathing isn't nearly as marketable.

♥

Those brief dates with Matt the painter made me feel better, or, really, just perfect enough. The day after, I always felt lighter on my feet, as if I really could accomplish the thirteen tasks on my list before my son got home from school, as if my makeup was just the right combination of dewy and dramatic, as if I too could pose on a red carpet and be the woman who other women wished with their whole bodies they could be. Perhaps I could have replicated this rush by buying cashmere or face oils or absurdly shaped sex toys, but I used Matt instead.

And with just a dating app on my phone, I could feel that high any time I wanted.

There was the man who looked like Anderson Cooper.

There was the man who was rude to the server at the bar.

There was the man whose sweet dog tried to sleep on top of me.

There was the man who was a banker but wanted to be a comedian. (He wasn't very funny.)

I knew, even then, that none of these men were permanent. Their presence was designed to be temporary, to distract me from the bald facts of my life, which were that I was a middle-aged woman floundering through self-loathing and the remains of a long marriage while trying to build a decent co-parenting relationship. These men told me I was beautiful. They held doors open for me. They looked at my body and didn't see the scars of childbirth or the ghost of my younger self. My job fascinated them. They said I had a nice home. I made them laugh.

I made divorce and the writerly life look easy. I wore flattering dresses, some with sparkles, and painted my mouth red or purple or fuchsia. I always knew which restaurant to try, or the latest play to see. I told them stories of my public writing life, including my first big literary festival, where I wore four-inch heels and a pencil skirt, only to trip and fall dramatically as I walked onto the stage. They might have thought I was sailing through single motherhood, as blithely as any famous actress. I let them believe it. I needed them to. Because their little hits of approval and desire bolstered me up just enough to get through another day of being someone I couldn't learn to love.

♥

In the years following, Miriam's husband would leave and direct his anger at her and, once, me. She would meet her own version of Matt, a man whose attraction to her was so obvious she couldn't ignore it, try as she might in giant puffer coats and baseball caps. The marriages of other friends would fall apart, and I shared as much information about the process as I could, referring them to my family lawyer, who oversaw the divorces for an entire group of women I was close to. They would all find their own Matts, men who smoothed over the transition between marriage and not-marriage, whose attention helped carry them through the deep pits of depression and the sad nights spent alone after their children had gone to bed. These men came over with wine, texted photos of their dicks, helped quiet the parts of my friends' brains that whispered, *You loser, look at the mess you've made. Why would anyone like you?* Undoubtedly, those men had their own agendas. Maybe they chose lonely, newly divorced women for a reason. Maybe they had their own inner voices to shush. But in the end, did it really matter? They did their jobs, and everyone was at peace with themselves for an evening, a day, maybe a few weeks.

♥

After almost three years, I decided to stop the carousel of hook-up dates. I went offline, had a bad boyfriend and then a good one, then went online again. I took the apps off my phone and only accessed them on my laptop, when I had time. I was settled in my new home, my new jobs, and happy with the life I had built by myself, but still I wondered if a real partner, a commitment, might be something

I could try for again. I saw my counsellor every week, and had even gone to a one-week mental health retreat, where I dug deep into the pain of my childhood, of always being the little kid left behind, lonely and scared. I learned that my all-consuming, crippling worry that I would become my mother was the exact thing that would prevent it from happening. "You already know this is possible," my counsellor said, "so I trust that you will do everything you can to never allow it."

Maybe I could be a good partner this time. Or at least I could try.

One night, a message appeared. A man named Jake made a joke, referencing a line in my profile where I had mentioned my love of musical theatre. I clicked on his photos, as one does, and scanned through a series of indistinct selfies taken in his car. I sent these to my friends, asking if they could tell what he looked like. No one really could. By then, I had developed a thick skin when it came to dating and men. Maybe I would meet this featureless man and it would work out. Or maybe it wouldn't, but I could shrug it off with a glass of wine and a YouTube makeup tutorial if I had to. It would be okay.

But you know how this will end. We met. I saw his ridiculously intense blue eyes. We fell in love.

None of it is perfect. We fight about scheduling, about our romantic pasts. He worries about my anxiety and depression. I worry that he takes on too much for his retired parents. We are both getting older, and we're acutely aware that living in a city where housing prices are astronomical could spell disaster if either one of us falls ill and is forced to stop working. He doesn't spell very well. I can't ever figure out how much to tip in a restaurant. When we are with friends, I do all the talking.

My therapist once told me that I only rage when the edges of my vulnerability are touched, when something threatens to poke the things that hurt the most. Often, it's about my success as a writer and the money I make, which is much less than what readers might think. Sometimes, it's about my mother. Once in a while, it's about my parenting.

The idea of Gwyneth pokes at all of those vulnerable spots, and I know the irritation that she elicits is blown up to an exaggerated, inappropriate size. It's her face, not mine, that appears on those movie screens, saving the world as Pepper Potts in the Marvel universe. It's Gwyneth who has built an empire worth millions and millions of dollars. Whatever success I think I might have, it will never be as lavish as hers. I don't think I'm even capable of dreaming that big. And if I can't dream it, then I've failed before I've started, which sounds like something a speaker at her wellness summit might say.

But failure is a natural part of the real-life mess we're all mired in, isn't it? Perfection isn't possible, not even for Gwyneth. If you pay attention to celebrity gossip writers, you have heard the same rumours I have, which whisper of the human wreckage hidden beneath the Goop sheen. Perhaps none of it is true, or all of it. What is almost certainly true is that selling aspiration demands maintaining a surface perfection, no matter what roils underneath.

I could tell you that when Jake came into my life, he swept away all of these complicated feelings about privilege and desire, lack and capitalism, but he didn't. Instead, he arrived, self-assured and rock-steady, at home in his body and his flaws, and that was enough.

Our life is small, and it centres on our kids and our weird rescue dog and going to happy hour whenever we can. Gwyneth's toned, silk-clad presence can hover over me all it likes, whispering, *You'll never have what I have, Jen. You're not valuable enough.* I still hear her. But what I have learned is that I need very little, and there is no rule that I must want more than I have. Toned thighs might be nice, but no one would see them. The vagina of my youth could be fun, but I am in my forties and it wouldn't even match.

♥

It was just a text. *Let's get together tonight.* It was from Matt the painter. By then, it had been over two years since I last saw him, and a year since I had met Jake. I stared at the message for a minute, before deleting it and his number from my phone. I heard myself laughing, with lightness, and I went on with my day.

THE
RAGE HOUSE

There is a rage that builds inside your body over time. You are an anxious girl, a good student, the editor of your high school yearbook, a hard worker who respects authority, even when the boss at your first real job yells at you about the petty cash box until you run to the washroom and cry in a stall. You tell people you are sad or worried or frustrated or annoyed, but never that you are angry because you are a good girl and good girls never feel anger. You don't know that the rage accumulates. You don't even register it, so quickly does it get buried underneath the tears and sad poems and everything you have to do in a day just to get on with things. But the rage grows, each new indignation sticking to an unwieldy ball of the old ones, a lump, uneven and crooked.

What it contains:

Every time your mother said you weren't pretty enough.

The junior prom when the boy you liked asked if he should ask out your best friend.

The professor whose only comment when he handed back your essay was that you should go back to your ESL classes.

That Beastie Boys concert when you were pushed to the front and sweaty young men pawed at your body until you couldn't tell how many hands were on you or who they belonged to.

The boyfriend who hissed insults at you at a reading and then drove away, leaving you to sign books while trying not to cry.

The neighbour's pit bull who attacked your dog so silently.

What happens when the rage becomes too big to be contained? You tear off your glasses and throw them at your mother. You walk in the December rain until your parka is soaked through but you are still burning hot. You punch a kitchen cupboard. You drink.

But these small eruptions release only the smallest amount of pressure. The misshapen lump is still there, gathering humiliations, never forgetting a slight, an assault, a lie. And still you don't acknowledge it exists. You carry on, parenting your son, walking the dog, writing books that dive deep into melancholia, into the desires that consume other people, and, yes, sometimes into anger. But it isn't yours. It's fiction.

All you ever do is hide behind the fiction. And it works. Until it doesn't.

You don't know this yet, but the big release, the one that projects demons and banshees and succubi into the world with terrifying velocity, is coming. You will not be ready. No one will be.

♥

Pop singer Sia on how she rages at herself and what that sounds like: "Um, mostly, 'Fat fuck, fat fuck, fat fuck. Tree trunk, tree trunk, fat fuck, fat fuck, tree trunk, tree trunk, loser, loser, fat fuck, loser, fat fuck, fat fuck.'"

♥

After a separation, there is silence, an unnerving quiet that settles over everything. If you've ever been in a long-term relationship that ended, you know that the nights and the early mornings are the worst for this. No one else flushes the toilet when you are trying to sleep. No one moves your glass of water on the bedside table. The radio is always on the station where you left it. No one grinds coffee until you do, eyes crusted with sleep, body untouched for twenty-four hours or forty-eight hours or however long it's been. Weeks maybe. Months sometimes.

In the silence that followed my separation, I learned to love Sia. It was 2015 and her bestselling album, *1000 Forms of Fear*, had been released the summer before, the summer that I knew, in a way that I hadn't yet dared to express in words, that my marriage was dying. I had heard "Chandelier," her breakout single, on the car radio as my then-husband was driving. He had made a face and changed the station.

The song, if you've never heard it, is *big*. It starts quietly enough, with Sia singing gently, a snare drum beating behind her voice like a party just getting started even as she chants, "Party girls don't get hurt, can't feel anything." She sings rhythmically through the bridge, a musical drinking game that has her counting what I've always imagined to be tequila shots. By the time we get to the chorus, Sia is howling, her voice careening like the wild swings of a chandelier at a party, a drunk girl clinging to its arms. Her soaring vocals are equal parts controlled and unleashed. She shouts about living fast and hard, about never once thinking about the future, and everyone has to believe her. Her voice cracks with sincerity.

Anger, when given the space, is always unremittingly honest.

In the summer of 2015, I played "Chandelier" on repeat, something I hadn't done with any song since I was in high school and playing "Brian Wilson" by Barenaked Ladies over and over again while I lay in bed, moping. I listened to Sia when I applied my makeup, when I took my first selfie for my OkCupid profile, when I changed my outfit four times while getting ready for my first real date in seventeen years.

But I also listened to it when I was panicking, when my breath felt like it was exploding from my chest, when my blood pressure was so high I could no longer see, the vessels behind my eyes pushing with their swollen, stretched-out walls.

I should clarify: I didn't turn on the song in the middle of an anxiety attack. I would turn it on whenever I felt dread creeping through my limbs, when the dead weight of it scared me, when I could accomplish nothing because I was pinned down by the worry, the sharp thoughts circling my brain like mad electrons. I was terrified of looking for housing, applying for a mortgage by myself, dividing a shared life and then packing up what remained, undressing in front of someone new with my childbearing body and its silvery stretch marks. All of that rendered me immobile—the heft, the bulk of rancid worry sitting on my chest.

But then Sia's voice, rising an octave, tearing a hole through the bassline, found its way to a release valve buried deep inside my body. Once triggered, I was on fire from the inside out. What I thought had been anxiety was a well-mannered pilot light until I heard her sing, "I'm holding on for dear life . . . won't open my eyes." That's when I knew my hold on this new life I was trying to create was just a grasp. There was no foundation for me, as there rarely is for women who leave a marriage, for women who are their children's primary care-givers, and whose careers have faded as they managed playdates and preschools. My son and I could slip and fall through the cracks at any minute, and that, above all else, felt like bullshit. I had a family, friends, a degree, professional colleagues. And yet I didn't know where I was going to live, how I was going to support myself or my child, what dark evil was waiting for me when I no longer had a husband to protect me.

What utter bullshit.

The rage burst into the air and it hurt. I ran to the bathroom and leaned against the door with my whole body so my son wouldn't accidentally walk in. If you had touched me, my skin would have burned yours clean off. But I needed to let the anger burn up the oxygen in the room, let it take my breath away with its oppressive heat, because by then the rage had been slowly gaining mass inside me for years. And it was time to release it into the world before it burned all of me away.

♥

It is the early 2000s and I am newly married, trying my best to fit into my husband's group of friends—almost all white, almost all men, almost all lawyers. Like many women of colour before me, I know how to read a room, observe the social dynamics, and then translate that into what I can say and do that will both allow me entry into a group and impress that group. For these men, it's relatively simple: drink a dark beer I don't like, yell about movies made by Tarantino or Scorsese or Anderson (both Wes and Paul Thomas), and never complain about how drunk and loud they get or how late they go home to their wives. I watch just enough NFL football to pretend I care.

I am good at this game. They say I'm cool. I start to believe I enjoy it.

(Behind my office door in the small downtown apartment I share with my husband, I write a novel about a family not unlike mine, and the sadness I feel about how the pain of immigration is forgotten, and the schisms between fathers and sons, mothers and daughters. I relive an old assault both in my head and in the pages of this novel that is so tender and exposing. But these are not the kind of things I discuss with these men.)

One Friday evening, we are on a bar patio by English Bay, the sun a warm liquid gold that settles on our heads, and I feel pretty, like the sun is an equalizer and there is no privilege, no inequities. I am lulled.

Someone asks me about Chinese food and restaurants, and I answer, excited, for once, to be asked about myself. My parents owned a small restaurant in the early 1970s with a view of English Bay. They had nice tablecloths and served chow mein and sweet and sour pork and Sunday roasts. There were pancakes and hash browns in the morning and wontons at lunch. My mother's cooking—elaborate and so thoroughly Chinese Canadian, as opposed to authentically Chinese—is one of my favourite topics. One of the men, a lawyer I don't know well, scoffs by saying, "Oh, come on, Jen. We all know you're just a banana anyway."

Have you ever felt rage rising in your body? Of course, you have. You know, then, that it is inexorable on bad days, or sensitive days, or when there is no hard shell to block its growth, only a thin dry membrane, easily punctured. You also know that it is pure heat, small flames licking at newspaper, burning as it builds in temperature, as it pushes closer and closer to the hand trying to contain it. When it reaches its destination, it's too late. Nothing will contain it.

I stand up. I shout. *"What did you just say no one gets to call me that Chinese Canadian identity isn't a fun game for white people go fuck yourself."*

He smirks. My husband and his friend pull me back down into my seat.

"It's not worth it," they say.

"Don't be mad," they say.

"Let me buy you a drink," they also say.

They coddle me. The smirking man does not apologize. He probably wouldn't even remember this incident. My anger is quickly doused, but the embers continue to burn, low and slow, long after.

♥

On the other side of rage is scorched earth. The remains of your feelings, all of your feelings, exist in only charred bits and pieces, some still smoking, others long gone cold and hard. You kick at some, pick up others. When you look around, you no longer see pinwheels of flame or a burning red sky, only clouds of grey ash. You hear, playing in a loop in your head, Sia's most ferocious song, "Fire Meet Gasoline," her voice singing, "When the fire dies, darkened skies, hot ash, dead match, only smoke is left . . . burn with me tonight."

You are forced to start over. Isn't the soil after a forest fire abundant in nutrients? Something will grow here, you tell yourself. Something better. You stomp through, shake the burnt detritus from your boots, looking for the right spot to stake a claim for your new, productive life.

♥

The day I moved into my tiny townhouse, I tried very hard not to cry. Four years earlier, my ex-husband and I had bought a 1920s-era house in a nice neighbourhood and spent a year and a half and a lot of money renovating it carefully, gently papering the plaster walls, adding insulation where there had only been emptiness and cold air. I loved that house, with its long yard and the Douglas fir that hosted a congress of shrieking starlings every September. We had bought it from the original owner, who had come to it as an eighteen-year-old bride, raised her children and grandchildren in it, and hung horseshoes over every entry. When we gutted the attic, I found a faded stack of Father Christmas stickers, a fake pearl necklace, stray buttons, and sequins that glimmered in the dark corners.

My townhouse was not that kind of home, but I tried to make it nice. I installed shiny chandeliers, hung art I had made when I was trying to be a photographer, chose baseboards as if baseboards mattered. I bought pristine new white sheets. All in an effort to conceal that I now lived in a cookie-cutter home, in a complex of twenty homes just like it. Same doors, same gas fireplaces, same nineties light switches.

Anger had brought me here, I reminded myself. I was mad that the marriage the world had promised me had imploded. I was mad that most job and residency opportunities for writers were impossible for a single mother and primary caregiver. I was mad I could afford so little in a city with skyrocketing real estate prices. I had packed in a rage, paid the movers in a rage, sold the big chaise that wouldn't fit in my new house in a rage.

That first night, I lay in my bed, surrounded by boxes, and stared at my bedroom ceiling. I was there alone, of course, as I had been for many nights since the separation, as I knew I would be for many nights to come. There was no one to help me break down boxes, vacuum the dirt the movers had tracked in, or throw away the packing foam that seemed to have wedged itself into every corner. I needed to put up curtains, organize the pantry, find my storage locker. My son was asleep in the next room. My dog was settled on her pillow. I couldn't leave and I was too tired to move.

I picked up my phone, found Sia, and pressed play.

In "Elastic Heart," one of the few songs on *1000 Forms of Fear* that leans into sadness, Sia yowls gently about a slow and inevitable heartbreak, as if she is exhausted. Walking through a scorched landscape can wear on a person. You clamber over uneven terrain and piles of your burnt past. You sink in where the ash is deep and soft. When you stop to think, the fatigue crashes over you, and you sit down on a still-warm boulder.

Here I was, in the House That Rage Built. And I didn't know when I would be angry again, if I was still capable of generating it, of caring.

And yet the possibilities of a new kind of life were all around me, some in boxes, some haphazardly piled on any shelf that fit. It was hard to imagine how anything in my home could be beautiful again, that I could choose paint or shingles with my old deliberate patience. It seemed futile. The townhouse was just a box. It could never be anything else.

But in the spring, when the sunshine warmed the tulip bulbs I had transported from my old house, the small planter would erupt, pink and yellow blooms brightening the shadows on my damp new deck. And as I drank my coffee in that quiet, in the calm blankness that comes from staring at top-heavy flowers bobbing in the breeze, there might be something else to catch fire and be angry about, something else to demolish and rebuild.

That first night though, I turned off the music, closed my eyes, and slept solidly until dawn, when the morning light spilled through my new window and my son crawled into bed with me.

THE
GENIUS

Winter in Vancouver is dark and wet. Raindrops sting when they hit your face. Clouds hover oppressively low in the sky, their black undersides sucking in light. That is, if there is light.

On an evening in January 2016, I was driving from the Abbotsford campus of the University of the Fraser Valley, where I was the writer-in-residence for the spring term, one of a number of jobs I was juggling at the time. Historically a farming community, Abbotsford is a small city just over seventy kilometres southeast of Vancouver. In the daytime, it's exactly as you would imagine: green fields, cows, intermittent housing developments populated by families who can no longer afford to live closer to downtown. In the strip malls, there are dollar stores, Indian buffets, children's clothing, discount shoes, an Olive Garden.

There is really only one way in and out of Abbotsford, and that's the Trans-Canada Highway, accessed through a series of roundabouts and on-ramps. I had learned to drive in the city, taking my test at seventeen at an urban licensing centre and acquiring most of my driving skills by cruising at twenty kilometres an hour down Robson Street—the famous luxury shopping strip where young people gather to gaze at the display windows and catcall each other. I could navigate heavy traffic on a main road riddled with stoplights. I could parallel park in front of a busy restaurant. What I had never done until that day was drive on the highway after dark. And I was petrified.

On the way to campus that morning, it had seemed easy, even in the greyness of daytime rain. I saw the signs; I followed the signs. I parked in a wide spot, paid the meter, and strode into my new office, right on time. As the day continued, as I met faculty and students and took a photo for my campus ID, I saw the light outside fading. It was January, after all, the time of year when the sun sets before five in the afternoon. I was scheduled to be there until six. My nerves prickled in my body and I started to sweat. When it was finally time for me to leave, I packed my bag, slung it over my shoulder, and walked to the parking lot, blinking hard and fast so I wouldn't cry.

As I steered the car toward the first roundabout, I tried to remember when I had to turn off, and whether I had to turn left or right. I'd spent weeks studying the route on Google Maps, but in my panic, I had forgotten everything. *Left*, I thought. *No, it's right. Shit, shit, shit.*

In the darkness, I took a wrong turn at the second roundabout and I was suddenly headed east on the highway instead of west. I was driving into Mission, another small city in the Fraser Valley, away from my home on the Burnaby-Vancouver border. I pulled over and turned on my GPS in desperation, something I had wanted to avoid because the voice prompts always made me more anxious than studying directions ahead of time. I started driving again, but I couldn't follow the calm female voice in time and found myself on an unlit road with a gas station and then a long stretch of trees and bush. If there were buildings behind me, I couldn't see them. I pulled over again, rested my forehead on the steering wheel, and cried. My son, then five and a half years old, was waiting for me at a friend's house, where her nanny had been looking after him since school let out at three. My elderly dog hadn't been outside since 9:15 that morning. And here I was stuck in Mission, with no idea how to get home.

I was crying because I was lost, but I was also crying for a specific loss. A year earlier, I had had a husband I would have called. He would have talked me out of my panic, found a way to help me get home, maybe even drove out to get me. Or he would have stayed home, calmly fed our son dinner, and taken the dog for a walk. He would have waited for me at the door with a glass of wine and told me I'd done a good job navigating my way back.

None of these possibilities were a real option for me anymore. The organization of my life, the practical considerations that form the foundation of an artist's career—that was all my sole responsibility now. I was the creative, but I was also the cleaner, the cook, the accountant, the chauffeur, the counsellor. I had to support my own writerly life because there was no one else to rely on. No Sophia Tolstoy. No Dorothy Wordsworth. Just Jen, lost in Mission.

I started the car again and drove toward a restaurant. When I walked in and asked the hostess for directions, I was still crying. She gave me a hug and said gently, "You can do this. I'm sure of it." She stood in the doorway and pointed at the highway overpass to the left. "See? That's where you have to go. It's easy."

But I wasn't convinced.

♥

In early 2020, the popstar Justin Bieber released a ten-episode documentary about, well, himself. Called *Justin Bieber: Seasons*, it was timed to help promote *Changes*, his first studio album in five years. During those years, he had become tabloid fodder for a string of bad behaviour—crashing a luxury car, urinating in a bucket in a restaurant kitchen, appearing sad and disengaged at his own concerts, throwing eggs at a neighbour's house in his elite Los Angeles neighbourhood, breaking up and getting back together and breaking up again with actress-singer Selena Gomez. None of these incidents was criminal (okay, maybe the egg throwing) or even all that bad on the spectrum of celebrities acting out. Instead, they were more irritating, the kind of frat-boy shenanigans that reek of wealth, entitlement, and boredom. The big difference, however, was that Justin Bieber is no anonymous frat boy.

As a child, Justin learned to busk on the streets of Stratford, Ontario, to help his family make ends meet. His sweet voice and puppy-dog eyes made him one of the first viral online stars. His talent was undeniable, so undeniable, in fact, that Scooter Braun, who was then an aspiring talent manager, flew thirteen-year-old Justin and his mother to Atlanta so he could meet, assess, and sign the musical prodigy after seeing him sing on YouTube. Soon, Justin was being mentored by the singer Usher, and he released his first studio album at the age of sixteen. His ascent to pop teen idol status was swift, raising not only his profile but that of everyone associated with him, especially Scooter Braun, who leveraged Justin's fame to attract other clients such as Ariana Grande, Black Eyed Peas, and Ashley Graham.

Justin was a teen idol in every sense of the word; even his floppy hair was famous. As he grew into adulthood, every move he made was predictably recorded by a crowd of paparazzi photographers and bystanders on their smartphones. And when he started to act out in public, videos of his bratty missteps ended up on social media and TMZ, triggering a public relations crisis. His fans were used to his cutest-boy-from-a-small-town persona, how he sweetly brought a girl up onstage at every concert when he sang "One Less Lonely Girl." By the time he was eighteen, he had personally—if not publicly— grown out of that image, and what he was doing was dismantling his previous persona far too quickly and far too destructively. He could alienate his fanbase and then he, and all the people he employed and supported, stood to lose a lot of money. They needed to perform damage control before it got any worse, before the albums stopped selling, before the ticket sales dropped.

Seasons has everything I love about how pop culture constructs its own narratives: a flawed but charming celebrity protagonist, a sad but scrappy origin story, a struggle with fame, and, at the end, a pretty wedding. There is never a moment when you're afraid the celebrity will not triumph. It isn't an exposé, like *Leaving Neverland*, the documentary about Michael Jackson and the allegations of child sexual abuse against him. It isn't fiction, like *A Star Is Born*, a film about an older Svengali who must die in order for his protegé to triumph. *Seasons* is a documentary about an artist's sense of self, about how Justin Bieber perceives his life, about what he has to believe in order to confront his deteriorating physical and mental health, while still continuing as a popstar and, somehow, as a regular person too. He can't be evil or fail or die. The happy ending is a certainty.

None of this is new. Historically, famous or accomplished or rich white men have been given second and third and fourth chances. In *Seasons*, I watched as Justin looked back at his troubled years, when he began to crumple under the weight of guilt and shame, his mental health struggles, and an ever-worsening relationship with his parents. He was, however, still making music and, most importantly, still making money. He even released a song titled "Sorry," possibly directed at his increasingly worried and disillusioned fans. There was no rock bottom for Justin, not really.

As I continued watching the docuseries, I found myself less and less interested in Justin's narrative of redemption. What I was watching for, instead, were the moments with Justin's wife, the model Hailey Bieber.

Throughout *Seasons*, the cameras follow Justin into the studio as he's recording *Changes*. Hailey is omnipresent, slouched in a chair, giving feedback when asked, listening to different versions of the same songs, but mostly she is silent, checking her phone but also never taking her eyes off him. "Honestly, I feel I'm here to cheer him on and support him," she says placidly to the camera. Later, she zips him into a portable hyperbaric chamber, which he climbs into periodically as a break from his creative work. She reminds him to take his medication, cajoling him when he resists. She bakes bread at their mansion in Ontario's lake country.

Does he use a Google calendar? Does he really have to when Hailey is there to take notes on his fatigue, his mental health, his moods, his diet?

He writes the music, records and performs the music, tours and promotes the music. Hailey takes care of everything else.

♥

It was 1998, and I was twenty-two years old, one of only two students of colour in my creative writing M.F.A. program in Montreal. I had not fit in from the very first day, when the program hosted a wine-and-cheese welcome reception and I sat in the corner of a couch, feeling small and making myself even smaller by sinking as deeply as I could into the cushions. Most of the other incoming students seemed to know what kind of wine they liked, holding their glasses by the stem and confidently walking around and greeting professors, not worrying about spilling on their white shirts. I was wearing plaid cargo pants.

I had just enrolled in a course called "The Canadian Novel and Historiography" and I didn't know what that meant, so I spoke to no one and only drank water. It didn't seem to matter that I, along with everyone else, had been accepted into this elite program on the strength of my writing, or that I had graduated from my bachelor's degree with first-class honours. The only person to approach me was Elaine, the other Chinese Canadian student, who told me she was from Scarborough and had never drunk wine in her life. *Thank god she's here*, I thought.

That first week, I submitted a poem for feedback in my workshop class, a poem that I had worked on for months and that had been through several rewrites. It wasn't a rough draft, quite by design, because I was too afraid of what people might have to say about a poem still in its infancy. When it was my poem's turn to be critiqued, the first person to speak was a male student sitting at the foot of the long table. "Here," he said, a copy of my writing in his hand. "I just rewrote your poem for you. That seemed like the most efficient thing to do."

I took the sheet from him and stared at the black ink of his confident handwriting. I wasn't angry; instead I looked at his suggestions and wondered if he was right, if he knew more about my poem than

I did. He acted like he was smarter than me, so perhaps he was. "Thank you," I said.

Later, as I walked thirteen blocks back to my bachelor apartment, I began to realize that what he had done was antithetical to all workshopping etiquette, and that he had assumed I was dumber and less talented than him. The rage grew and I stopped, pulled his version of my poem out of my backpack, and tossed it into a garbage can on Maisonneuve. Two months later, I dropped out altogether, driven by depression and an acute sense of otherness, and I returned to Vancouver, moving back in with my mother. I stayed with her for just over a year, before getting married and moving to a downtown apartment where I would write the first drafts of my first novel. But I did not write poetry again for fifteen years.

♥

We've all heard about how indispensable Sophia Tolstoy was to her novelist husband, the fiery and ideologically rigid Leo Tolstoy. Only she could decipher his handwriting, and it was she who transcribed and edited *War and Peace* seven times, even as she alone cared for their thirteen children, managed the household, and provided support to the peasants who lived on their land. She is the epitome of the long-suffering, dutiful, creative man's wife, and she wasn't—isn't—the only one.

There was Véra Nabokov, who—in addition to performing all of the domestic duties so Vladimir could prolifically write his novels, short stories, plays, criticism, and poems—prevented her husband from burning the manuscript for *Lolita*, his most famous work.

Cynthia Dunbar, Henry David Thoreau's mother, brought him food and washed his clothes while he famously lived in a cabin a short walk from his family home and wrote *Walden: A Life in the Woods*, his treatise on living alone and simply. And Dorothy Wordsworth not only lived and worked for her brother William, but also emotionally and creatively supported William's friend, Samuel Taylor Coleridge. If you squint just the right way, these women could be muses, if we're being generous.

The creative genius and the art they produce are a funny form of social currency. In order to build a career, the genius has to *produce* something, whether a book or a film or a painting, and the necessary focused attention to create requires care and time and nurturing. Either the genius makes the space for themselves, or relies on someone else to make it for them. Leo Tolstoy could not have written *War and Peace* without Sophia taking care of everything else so he could write, grow a beard, and ruminate on his religious convictions. Justin Bieber couldn't finish *Changes*, which he wrote as a tribute to his love for Hailey Bieber, without her calm, practical presence. Or so the women themselves had to believe.

As a writer, I am often invited to appear at literary festivals. When I was an emerging author, I would lurk in the festivals' hospitality suites, all but invisible to the more famous authors around me. In those moments, as someone who had been so recently granted entry into a very exclusive and privileged space, I was at once a member of this authorial group but also not. My youth, my femininity, my small physical size, and my race combined to form a kind of cloaking device that kept others from recognizing me as a fellow writer. It was far more common for other authors to assume I was a publicist or a server or a girlfriend. While those with more fame and power barely saw me, I never stopped seeing them.

There was the bestselling novelist who controlled his peers and students with a strange combination of nurturing and cruelty, who held court at the local festival, always surrounded by a crowd of women ready to laugh at his jokes. There was the prize-winning author who brought his wife and toddler to a literary party only to ignore them both while she tried to nurse amid all the noise, her shirt unbuttoned crookedly. There was the charming, handsome writer who challenged a series of attractive women to arm wrestle him in a bar, while his wife stayed home in a distant city.

The women took care of the house, the children, those male egos, their drinks. I know. I saw them.

♥

It's midnight and the only light glowing in my bedroom is my reading lamp. My dog Molly, now twelve years old, is on her orthopedic bed, paws up in the air, snoring. My bed is littered with research materials: *The Journals of Susanna Moodie* by Margaret Atwood, a biography of River Phoenix, an old *Interview* magazine yellowed at the edges, my battered spiral-bound notebook with pages and pages of fragments and ideas written in pencil. I am on deadline for two books. In the next room, my son is finally, finally asleep.

Earlier that day, I was on a school bus, supervising a field trip for his grade one class. When we returned home, I had to walk the dog, make dinner, help my son in the shower, read him a story, and cuddle him to sleep. He woke up three times before midnight with growing pains, and each time I closed my laptop and tried to lull him back to sleep. The three hours I usually have to write after his bedtime have disappeared. But my deadlines are still very much alive.

Just one more paragraph, I whisper to myself. And then when that paragraph is done, I say it again. *Just one more paragraph*. I write lines and immediately forget them. I worry that if I blink too much, I will just fall asleep, my head leaning back on the wall, laptop still lighting my face.

Tomorrow, I will have to get up at six, make breakfast, have a shower, gulp down a lukewarm coffee, walk my son to school, take the dog to the park, and then back home to prepare for my evening online class. I know if I don't take a nap, I will never make it through the two-and-a-half-hour workshop, where I am asked to give feedback on student writing and manage the feedback my students give to one another. I can already feel the anxiety in my stomach as I run through my planned day, looking for twenty-minute gaps when I can lie down and shut off my brain. It's only twenty minutes. But when do I ever have twenty minutes?

I write one more paragraph.

The next morning, when my son runs into my room at dawn, the books and magazine have fallen to the floor, and my laptop is balanced precariously on a pile of other books on my nightstand. I don't remember if I saved my work, but I have to get up. I have to manage.

♥

The male literary genius is a very particular archetype because of its rarity. It takes a lot to be considered a creative genius—a perfect storm of fan adulation, critical acclaim, and commercial success. If the man is irritable or a hermit or writes scathing reviews of his enemies' books; if he dresses terribly or drinks too much or leaves his wife for an undergraduate student twenty years his junior, the genius label still fits. In fact, it fits even better.

There have always been female literary geniuses too, but most creative women have historically had to manage their creative lives alongside their families and homes and finances. Carol Shields actively mothered five children while writing her fiction, assigning herself a daily quota of two pages for the one and a half hours she had free. Mary Shelley wrote the earliest examples of speculative fiction in English even as she endured the deaths of three of her children and her husband, Percy Bysshe Shelley, whose literary estate she would go on to manage. Toni Morrison raised two children as a single mother while making space for Black authors as an editor at Random House, writing her seminal and prize-winning books, and teaching at Princeton University. All three of these women are considered geniuses. Their work—canonized and elevated—is, without a doubt, extraordinary. *The Stone Diaries* taught me that an epic novel can be comprised of detail and quiet. *Frankenstein* showed me that the darkest impulses of the human soul, as written by a woman, could be thrillingly beautiful. And *The Bluest Eye* illuminated stories that had previously been obscured in the shadows, told in the crystal-clear voices of Black women and children in the years after the Great Depression. None of these female authors have reputations for the kind of bad behaviour we've long associated with genius. If you could ask them about the cliché of the untamed, irascible genius, I imagine they would reply, in a matter-of-fact tone, *Who has the time to misbehave?* And then they would laugh before answering their own rhetorical question, *Only the men do, obviously.*

The difference, of course, is that these female writers were not geniuses to the exclusion of their domestic lives. Rather, their genius was required to fit into the rest of their lives. They created space, they compartmentalized, they managed and *made do.*

♥

It was 2014. I had escaped to the basement of the Depression-era house my ex-husband and I were trying to renovate, even as our marriage was beginning to fray at the edges. Upstairs the house was a construction zone, with pipes and ducts sticking out of the kitchen walls while we waited for new appliances. My son was finally asleep in his big-boy bed and I was exhausted. All I wanted was silence in the dark cave of the basement, where I could stare at the concrete blocks if I wanted to. I was hunched on an old pullout couch, a blanket over my shoulders, when I opened a notebook, intending to write a journal entry, as my therapist had been encouraging me to do. But instead, as my pencil hit the page, what emerged was a poem. At first, I felt the gears in my head straining against the rust, as if the poetry inside me had been buried, piled high with dust and cracker crumbs. But it was a poem. And my fingers burned with the writing of it.

As I kept writing over the next several months, the poems grew, into long, unwieldy lines, into narratives that circled in on themselves before ending with no real conclusions, no linear logic. They were nothing like the short epigrammatic pieces I had written in my twenties; after all, my life since then had stretched out twice as long. Even my body had stretched with pregnancy, only to be left soft and over-extended after childbirth. The poems would have to match. I pushed forward, long line after long line. I was thirty-eight and, for the first time in many years, the poems were straining to get out.

♥

When I was in my twenties, I read Elizabeth Smart's semiautobiographical novel, *By Grand Central Station I Sat Down and Wept*, and I loved it, hard. I still do.

I should clarify: *By Grand Central Station* isn't precisely a novel. It's a dizzying, internally dramatic, emotional prose poem that centralizes love against a backdrop of plain, hard-working life, as if the world is inhospitable to the passion the unnamed narrator feels for her married lover. When the couple is arrested in Arizona for adultery (the book was published in 1945), the narrator juxtaposes the police officer's direct and invasive questions with her own lyrical thoughts, styled after the Biblical Song of Songs. "When did intercourse first take place?" the officer asks, to which the narrator replies, "The king hath brought me to the banqueting house and his banner over me was love." Literally and figuratively, the real world, as depicted in this book, cannot understand or contain open and expressive female desire. And this is what I have always loved about *By Grand Central Station*.

The narrator loves a poet who will never leave his wife. She bears his child and raises her alone. She writes in fits and starts because of the child, but still she loves the poet, against all reason. She knows there are other choices, other men, other ways to live, but she chooses this path, because it's what her heart/body/mind truly wants, and she accepts the consequences.

It's hedonistic, in a way, to choose to live your life how you want despite how it will affect your finances, your family, your prospects. Elizabeth Smart, as well as her narrator, chose a love that was ostensibly free of restrictions. In real life, George Barker, her one true love, remained married even as Elizabeth bore four of his children as his mistress. They had an eighteen-year relationship that defied social rules.

Elizabeth's writing reflects this wild hedonism; George Barker himself called *By Grand Central Station* a "Catherine wheel of a book." As exhilarating as it is, I always come away from it with a sense of exhaustion. In this life, in this world, a fetterless love might be an ideal, but it's also never real, and there are very tangible costs. In the end, after the children, after the broken promises, after struggling for money, Elizabeth's love for George wasn't free or liberating at all, but exactly the opposite. It came with restrictions and disappointments, irrevocable ones. He abandoned her in a Paris hotel room with their four children when he discovered he couldn't pay the bill. Her relationship with her family was fractured because of her insistence on continuing this affair, and Elizabeth fell in and out of contact with her relatives for years. Once, she rode a moped through a windstorm just to see him for a few hours.

But worst of all, by far, was this: after *By Grand Central Station* was published, she wouldn't publish again for thirty-two years.

Elizabeth Smart made choices that are difficult for many to understand, including me. But then, so did George Barker, and his career did not suffer. She may have been an irascible genius, but she was also the responsible mother, the one who put aside her art for over three decades to just *get it done*. Even Elizabeth Smart, with her unruly, genius heart, had to get on with the business of life, and that life came first.

♥

"I've seen a change in Justin since Hailey came into his life. I think any man finds a good woman he's going to have a good change. Justin is a better man because he married Hailey."
SCOOTER BRAUN, *JUSTIN BIEBER: SEASONS*

"I sleep great now that Justin is married and she's around. Not only because I don't worry about what call I'm going to wake up to, which is what the case was five years ago. But also because I know that someone is there with him if something goes wrong. There's this very confident, capable, smart adult that is there to help him with it. And I also know he's much happier than the Justin Bieber five years ago."
ALLISON KAYE (JUSTIN'S GENERAL MANAGER), *JUSTIN BIEBER: SEASONS*

The trope of the troubled male genius who is self-destructive and unmoored without the help of a supportive, indefatigable woman is hard to ignore when you watch *Seasons*. All ten episodes are structured to present Justin Bieber as a lost boy.

Justin seems happy, but in interviews he talks about his childhood as the only son of a struggling young single mother, how they
lived in subsidized housing and took refuge with his grandparents
when the money ran out. He rarely mentions his father, and their
relationship is spotty and tenuous.

The peak of his hurt child story comes when, after years of success, Justin begins to act out at the age of eighteen. After an arrest for
drag racing on a public street, his mugshot appears on the front pages
of newspapers and gossip blogs. Grainy footage of him smoking
weed and verbally assaulting a photographer is uploaded to the internet and viewed thousands of times.

If YouTube and social media created Justin Bieber, it was also
starting to destroy him.

Members of his management team, many of whom are interviewed for *Seasons*, begin to worry. Some distance themselves from
the train wreck. Others dive in and try to manage his every waking
moment. His security guards check his pulse every morning, as one
imagines must have been done for other troubled pop stars like
Whitney Houston, Amy Winehouse, Jim Morrison. If Justin's parents, separated and acrimonious, try to support him during this time,
it's never mentioned. It is also never mentioned whether he supports
them financially, although in the few shots we see of them, they are
well-dressed and professionally styled, no longer the small-town kids
struggling to find work.

Finally, after he turns twenty-one, Justin gets sober, but his body
and brain are still in chaos. He sees doctors and is diagnosed with
Lyme disease, Epstein-Barr, and anxiety. He is trying to get better,
staying out of the public eye, unsure he will ever perform again.

And then Hailey returns to his life.

The couple first met in 2009—Justin was fifteen and Hailey thirteen—when her father, the actor Stephen Baldwin, introduced them backstage at *The Today Show*. Years later, they started dating, only to break up during the most tumultuous era of Justin's life, when smartphone videos of him standing on a bar top and slamming back tequila had become an unsurprising spectacle on *Entertainment Tonight*.

In 2018, during a quiet period when Justin wasn't touring or recording music, he sees her on *The Tonight Show with Jimmy Fallon*, promoting a documentary about social media and modelling. With a high, cheerleader-esque blonde ponytail and a leather mini-skirt, she performs a party trick: opening a beer bottle with her teeth. The next day, he calls her and asks to reconnect. Two months later, he proposes in the Bahamas.

Hailey has always been beautiful, with blonde hair and dark eyes and a finely postured body. Although she has worked for big brands like Calvin Klein and Ralph Lauren, she is not the most successful model, especially compared to some of her friends and contemporaries like celebrity models Kendall Jenner and Cara Delevingne, who come from similarly privileged backgrounds. She has the time to be there for Justin while he records, promotes, and tours his music. Her presence seems to unlock a peaceful, contented Justin. She is— according to him, his two managers, as well as his creative director— steady, stabilizing, nurturing, and responsible. She is a devout Christian, as he has tried to be, off and on. In short, she is everything he has always needed. When she became engaged to Justin, she had just left a relationship with the younger, fresher Canadian pop heartthrob, Shawn Mendes. There is no question: in these overlapping celebrity circles, Justin is by far the biggest star. And there is no question that both he and Hailey know it.

Their first wedding is a quickie courthouse ceremony; their second, a year later, is at a sprawling estate in South Carolina with celebrity guests such as Kendall and Kylie Jenner, Usher, and Joan Smalls in attendance. Soon after, Hailey appears on the cover of *Elle*, in a fresh white romper, backlit by sunshine. The headline reads, "The Secret Life of Mrs. Bieber." Her birth name, Hailey Rhode Baldwin, appears nowhere. To the world, Hailey herself has ceased to exist. Mrs. Bieber has taken her place.

♥

"You are someone I look up to as an artist because you just keep going. You're a tank. You make it happen."
TEXT MESSAGE FROM BEN RAWLUK
TO JEN SOOKFONG LEE

Over the years, I have been told I am reliable, prolific, consistent. My books are well reviewed, but I have never won a literary prize or been considered for any awards that honour a career. I write good books that sell just fine. Nothing more, nothing less.

If people praise my career, it's for my hard work, my ability to move between genres, my empathy and activism in the community. The word *genius* has never been applied to me, but I never expected it would.

Most mornings, my son and I wake up by seven. I take the dog out to pee, then I make breakfast, then my son's school lunch, all the while listening to the news on the radio and taking gulps of quickly cooling coffee. Then I have a shower, get dressed, and walk to school with my son and the dog. Afterward, I walk to the dog park, where she runs with her friends, tail wagging, sometimes eating mud in the off-leash field. When I return home, I clean up the dirty dishes, put in a load of laundry, and work out. By the time I sit down to write, it is eleven o'clock. That gives me three hours and forty-five minutes before I have to go back to school for pickup. My son and I do his homework together before I make dinner. We eat, I do the dishes, then we walk the dog one last time. While my son has a shower, I wash my face and brush my teeth. We read a story together. He is asleep by nine. Sometimes I stay up until eleven to watch makeup tutorials or cooking shows. Often, I fall asleep instead.

What I didn't include: time spent teaching or preparing to teach, editing, attending community events and committees, seeing my friends, managing my relationship with my partner. Those tasks fit into pockets of time that are measured in minutes, not hours.

If anything goes wrong, my entire life has to readapt, moving like mercury around new barriers, spreading over days instead of only one, pushing the fun moments out of the way.

In 2019, I accidently became pregnant. I was forty-two years old and my partner Jake was forty-nine. His son was sixteen, mine was eight. My home is a small two-bedroom townhouse, just big enough for an adult, a child, and a small dog. Jake's place was even smaller, in a high-rise twenty minutes away. We had been planning to move in together, but we both knew we were at least a year or two away from blending our children and lives. A baby would accelerate everything and we didn't know if we could keep up.

In the end, I decided to terminate the pregnancy. Before the abortion, I cried every single day, imagining the face of the baby I could be having. I was convinced she would be a girl, and I would have named her Daphne. She would be little, as I had been, as Jake had been as a child. She would learn to walk early, and then run, to keep up with her older brothers and so she could chase the dog. I believed in her. I saw her when I closed my eyes.

But I also knew that there was no room for us to live as a five-person family in the most expensive real estate market in Canada. I couldn't take time off because when I don't work, I don't get paid. Our sons might love her, or they might be jealous, the two of them already feeling tenuous in their positions. We would have to move to the Fraser Valley, or cram ourselves into something far too small. Jake and I would be exhausted, far enough into our midlife that a new baby would drain us of any extra energy. I wanted a baby. I didn't want a baby. I spent hours lying on the couch, running that infuriating thought through my head like a nursery rhyme, but for a baby I would lose.

I couldn't write. I taught as little as possible. I stopped cleaning the house. I told only a handful of people I was pregnant. I didn't answer emails. I stared out the window at my tiny deck, off which a toddler could fall and then tumble down a concrete staircase, down to the concrete sidewalk below.

The abortion, which happened on a Friday, was uneventful, painless, relieving even. I spent two days resting. On Monday, I was back at work, back managing my son's field trips and swimming lessons. A house guest came to stay with me for a few days. I was still bleeding, still cramping, but it didn't matter—I had to play catch-up. In the weeks following, I only allowed myself to cry at night in bed, my dog's warm body tucked behind my knees. Somehow, nothing in my life was different, and the lack of an acknowledgement that something momentous had happened felt unfitting and cruel. I had been pregnant with a baby I could have loved or resented, and now I no longer was, but there was no ceremony, no meal I could make that would mark this moment of loss and not quite loss.

Within a week, I had caught up on my work. I met my deadlines, sent apologetic emails, rescheduled meetings. My grief had been smoothed over. My life was organized by me, yet again.

♥

In episode six of *Seasons*, Justin is standing at the mouth of a desert cave near the Amangiri resort in Utah. The rocks and sand are orange, and Hailey sits at the top of a crudely built staircase, shaded by the cave's overhang. Justin begins to sing with his hands over his eyes, and his voice, still crystal clear and strong, echoes around them both. When he is done, Hailey cheers.

"Do I sound good?" he asks, his speaking voice tentative, so unlike his confident singing just moments before.

"Hell yeah, baby," she shouts, a wide smile on her face.

"Okay," he says, quiet in the desert.

If I were Hailey, I would also stick around, watching from the sidelines, providing the occasional burst of cheerful support. I would count the pills and zip up the hyperbaric chamber without complaint, curl into a corner of the studio, and text my sister her daily horoscope. I would go home and plan our meals for the week, making sure that Justin's diet supports his health, even though all he wants is an In-N-Out burger with fries. I would smile and make nice with his parents, all the while thinking they had spectacularly failed him and that was why I needed to mother him now. I would wait. Because time could change everything.

When the album was done, I would ask for time to travel for modelling jobs. I would hire a personal chef, program Justin's phone with reminders to take his medication, make sure his assistant knows how to manage his breaks and his counselling sessions. I would clear the house of any junk food, checking for drugs or alcohol along the way. When I left, I would kiss him at the front door and take an Uber by myself, so he feels grounded at home. Airports are hard. No one likes to be the one left behind.

If all of this happens the way I had planned, perhaps for the next album or the next panic attack, he wouldn't need me as much anymore. Perhaps we could be like other couples and share the household work, the social management, the tasks that will proliferate when we have children. That could be the long-term goal.

But for now, I would do just as Hailey is doing. I would watch and wait and smile, chat about my husband on every talk show even though I am promoting my own project. I would try to look pretty so he has something nice to look at. I would do it all.

The quiet precedes the emancipation.

♥

For years, I had been working solely on novels and published three in nine years. It was a pace I couldn't maintain forever, especially when the divorce was unfolding, especially when I was anxious and depressed, brittle to the core with parenting, work, and searching for housing. Poems seemed less daunting, episodic, the perfect length for my brain, which was frantically running in circles every single day, to focus on.

The poems were not, oddly, about my failing marriage or my ex-husband. They were about the long aftermath of divorce, about the ways in which women, freed of the responsibilities of a relationship, may find themselves floundering, unsure of their own individual ambitions or needs. We know what the people we choose to love want. We know how they like their eggs, the best time to ask them a hard question, what to say when they are angry. We spend so much time caring for others—being wives or mothers or dutiful daughters or good employees—we often no longer know what we want.

I would start a poem, and the wants, the desires, would come rushing out and onto the page.

I wanted late nights and long dates, slutty clothes and the surprise of a touch on the small of my back, cheap wine and fine cheese, midnight snacks and fuzzy mornings. I wanted my own house, sparkly light fixtures, wallpaper that glimmers in the dawn, a window that feels like an opening. I wanted solitude, but only sometimes. I didn't know I had wanted so many things. And I didn't know that so many of these desires had been lying under the surface, submerged by marriage and responsibility, for so long.

I have written poems for most of my life. They were my first literary love, the genre I went to school for, the way I processed my thoughts, until that graduate class stunned the poems into silence. Through an accident of creativity, I wrote my first novel, and then people asked for the second, and then it was all I knew how to write. I feared writing poetry for fifteen years, but as my outer shell as the respectable lawyer's wife began to crack and then fall away, what emerged was not another novel, but poetry. New poems, angrier poems, poems that shouted their words into the air, demanding space.

Poetry doesn't make money. Collections don't become bestsellers. If you write poems, it's because you want to. It's because they demand to be written. To rearrange your life and make sacrifices so you can carve out that writing time for something so impractical, it defies sense. But maybe you would bathe the children or cook a week's worth of meals for someone else, if you really believed in them.

It was only me, counting down the minutes until my son went to bed so I could write, buying the smallest desk at IKEA to squish into the one free corner of my bedroom so I could do something that was wildly impractical. It's a move a genius might pull, if she really believed in herself.

THE
HOMELAND

ONE

It is 1984, the summer I turn eight years old. My parents and I have flown to Hong Kong, where we visit with my mother's large, complicated family, leaving my sisters at home to tend to their summer jobs and boyfriends. My grandmother, who cared for me as a baby in Vancouver before returning to Hong Kong, is declining from complications of diabetes. We are there to say goodbye and to provide respite for the relatives who have been caring for her for months.

There are uncles, aunties, half-uncles, cousins, and half-cousins, a sprawling web of relatives who are connected by my grandfather's three wives, or more precisely, one wife and two concubines. Some are wealthy, if they happen to be the male children and grandchildren of the first wife. Some are decidedly not. My mother's brother lives with my grandmother, who was the third and youngest wife, in an apartment up six flights of winding stairs, a climb we make several times a day as we haul groceries—ingredients for medicinal soup, live chickens, as many greens as we can find—that will fortify my grandmother's health. When my parents and I collapse at night, all three of us sharing a single mattress in the middle of the living room floor, we sleep soundly and silently, the ceiling fan pushing the humid air above. Our first night, my uncle drinks too many beers, offering sips to his two daughters as if that were funny and not a sign of bravado masking fatigue and grief. After he stumbles to bed, my mother whispers, "He was always the troubled son."

My grandmother stays in her room, mumbling to herself and calling me by my sister's name whenever I am forced to sit on a small stool at her bedside and talk to her.

My two cousins dance to Canto-pop in their bedroom and practise their English with me. The younger one, June, resents my height and knockoff Esprit clothing, and she tells me that I am fat as often as possible. One night, she argues with me about which one of us is prettier, and my shrugs of disinterest enrage her. She runs out of the living room and returns with a chef's knife held high above her head, shouting, "I'm going to kill you!" When she rushes me, my father grabs her by the neck of her nightgown and my mother pushes me into a bedroom, where I cry, shivering in the hot damp air.

"Listen to me," my mother says. "Do not make a fuss. We are guests here."

When I see June the next morning, she is calmly eating her morning congee. I sit down beside her and take a cube of mango off the platter of cut fruit. She doesn't ask how I am. Instead, she says, "Mama says it's fine if we use the stereo today." We make plans to record an audio play and I pull a pad of paper toward me, writing lines of dialogue about an alien invasion. We make cassette copies and promise to keep them forever. We never speak about the knife again.

A week later, my parents and I take a train into Mainland China, to Guangzhou, the city nearest my father's home village. In a suburb, my aunt—the only one of my father's sisters who remained in China—lives in a five-hundred-square-foot house with her husband, daughter, and three children, although it's not clear to me if the children are distant cousins sent to live there from another city, or if they are all directly related. When we arrive, walking through unmarked narrow streets that lead past other houses, I smell pig shit and stare with alarm at the sticky black mud ringing my sandals. I can hear chickens and women shouting at their children.

My aunt's house has a dirt floor. There are no bedrooms, only this one square space with the kitchen in the corner and bedrolls stacked on the back of a sofa. My cousins have put on their best clothes for our visit, but even so they are a mishmash of patterns and fabrics; the skinniest one with the wide smile wears a yellow floral dress with a purple cardigan, missing a button, and clear jelly shoes, kept meticulously clean. The children are covered in mosquito bites, or maybe they're another kind of bite. I can't tell. Some of the sores are bleeding; others are scabbed over. I find myself scratching a ghost sympathy bite on my elbow.

Later, my parents take everyone out for dinner at the restaurant in our hotel. The meal is, as is appropriate for a family reunion like this, ten courses, the best my parents can find in Communist China. My relatives eat and eat, grabbing at the shared plates in the middle of the table so quickly that I don't bother trying to scoop any of it for myself. *I'm fat anyway*, I think to myself. When my cousins come up to our room afterward, they are fascinated with the bathroom, flushing the toilet over and over again, turning the taps on and off, marvelling at the hot and cold water, ignoring the toys I'd brought from Canada to give them—an Etch A Sketch, skipping ropes, bubble wands. I watch their glee as they splash water on one another, their clothes darkening with each spray. I bring in a colouring book and an unopened box of markers, but they ignore me, their feet now submerged in the bathtub. So I retreat and fall asleep on my bed alone with a crossword puzzle on the covers beside me.

That September, when I return to school in Vancouver, my teacher asks how our trip was. I want to tell her that my extended family had never seen running water before, that they took all the soap and towels from our hotel, that I alternately wanted them to play with me and stay far away, and that everywhere I went, adults asked, "Why is she so big? Why is her Chinese so bad? What are you feeding her?" I felt like an obtrusive Canadian grizzly bear, stomping through the crowds of tiny people in Hong Kong and Guangzhou, unwittingly knocking down neat displays of produce and causing panic among the small residents on their spindly bicycles. Everyone else in my class went camping at Manning Park or Alice Lake or, if they were lucky, took an airplane to Disneyland. I am dreading the questions she will inevitably ask. I will have to explain and explain and explain, and the only thing the layers of explanation would clarify is that my family—and our Chinese-ness—is *strange*.

I look up at my teacher's smiling face. "It was nice," I say. "The wonton noodle soup was really good. And my aunt bought me a Cabbage Patch Kid." I do not mention that I contracted food poisoning from the soup, or that the doll is a knockoff, its cheap fabric skin sparking with static whenever I try to hug it.

I am learning to self-edit, tailoring my stories to be simple, non-challenging constructions that skim the surface of what being Chinese Canadian means. These are not lies—not exactly—but amalgams of truth and not truth, designed to hide the persistent feeling that my family and I belong nowhere. It's easier this way. And it's a skill I will use again and again, for the rest of my life.

♥

In the 1980s, when I was a school-aged child growing up in relentlessly diverse East Vancouver, my friends and I asked each other the same question in playgrounds and classrooms: *What are you?* The answer was always Fijian or Native or Italian or Japanese. No one ever said Canadian, a word used only by the blondest kids, the ones who brought ham and cheese sandwiches to school, instead of a Thermos filled with noodles or curry. We never discussed the distinction. It was obvious.

Adults also bluntly asked *What are you?* and even as a child it was clear to me that the question was meant to impose a kind of order to the politics people kept in their heads. Eventually, the inevitable question became more sinister: *Where are you really from?* For me and the racialized people I am close to, this is the most dreaded question a white person could ask, precisely because it presupposes that where we are—here, in Canada—can't possibly be our real home, and that the genuine answer is simple, the name of a country that will magically settle all confusion.

There is rarely enough time to provide a fulsome explanation of how we see ourselves. If there was, I would say that my family initially came to Canada in the late 1800s, but because of discriminatory immigration policies, poverty, and war, my sisters and I were the first to be born here. I would also say that, for generations, we bought into the myth of Canadian multiculturalism, peace, and prosperity without knowing how that myth was built upon the genocide of Indigenous communities. I would say that the hierarchy of white supremacy has materially benefited my family but has also encouraged unquestioning acceptance of the unwritten rules imposed by whiteness, which include impossibly strict codes of behaviour and laughably simple categories that no one individual or group could ever fit into. As Asian North Americans, my family was taught to behave, to learn verbatim what was fed to us at schools and workplaces, and to never, ever complain. In return, we were promised jobs, relative safety, and the opportunity to help the migration of our relatives. I would say that these respectability politics have only protected me so much and the promises of safety and opportunity have never really been fulfilled. I would say that internalized white supremacy is a hard and unsustainable bargain that requires silence and acquiescence and leads, eventually, to self-loathing. And it leads to the suppression of dissent and raises barriers to the community fully engaging politically.

Finally, I would say that I am here, now, a Chinese Canadian woman, the simplest iteration of who I might be.

The idea of Canada imposes. It's eternal and persistent, evident in how we anglicize our names, how our restaurants dumb down the spices for a white palate, how cultural celebrations like Lunar New Year or Diwali are considered exotic, even though they are celebrated by millions of Canadians.

And yet even now, after writing about Chinese diasporic identity for most of my adult life, my grasp on what it means to be Chinese is slippery at best. You see, I could talk all day about how my identity is grounded in Canada, in the very specific ways I interact with people in Vancouver, where different communities collide every day. The most difficult part of my identity for me to grasp is the concept of being *Chinese*. The Canadian part has always been evident and tangible; it's everywhere: on television, in the newspapers, part of what we learned in school. My Chinese-ness, on the other hand, has had to fit into smaller spaces, the ones left behind. And it resisted.

♥

My family's history in Canada is inextricably tangled up with the history of twentieth-century China. As my grandfather prepared to leave his homeland for Canada in 1913, the Republic of China was newly formed and the entire identity of his home country was shifting, hurtling toward a modern republic after centuries of fractured feudalism, leaving rural families like ours behind to grapple with poverty and lack of opportunity. My grandfather's decision to come to Canada was a leap into the unknown, but, for him anyway, the risk was worth the gamble. During the four decades he lived alone in Vancouver, running his barbershop and sending money back to his family, China was invaded by Japan and spent years as one of the key battlegrounds of World War Two. Once Canada's Chinese Exclusion Act was lifted in 1947, my father, grandmother, and aunties began to emigrate, one by one, fleeing the Communist Revolution that had become an inexorable wave and would go on to kill millions while pitting neighbours against neighbours.

By the time I was born in 1976, all of this felt like ancient history, memories that my grandparents and parents never spoke about, focusing instead on buying a piano, planning a road trip to Disneyland, and planting a pink and red rose garden. I get it. Reliving the past is exhausting, an exhumation of feelings that get in the way of living a simple, happy life.

And yet, as I grew older, I noticed that anything that happened in China seemed to reverberate across the world to poke at the carefully constructed Canadian lives my family had built. Each time, we were reminded that our self-defined identity was not real to anyone else, that who we thought we were was fragile, susceptible to politics, scandal, and the old racist perceptions that never died but bubbled up over and over again.

Where are you really from?

June 4, 1989

My family watches the news, anchored by Tony Parsons, on television every night. His voice is newsroom serious, but his face, soft along the edges and framed by dark hair, reminds me of my father. On this night, we watch pro-democracy protestors, mostly students, peacefully protest in Beijing's Tiananmen Square. The tanks roll in. Soldiers fire into the crowd. The students scatter, but not before thousands die. It's the first time I see people who look like me engaged in protest and pushing for political change. We witness the lone young man standing in front of a line of tanks, only his body preventing them from advancing on crowds of students. My heart drops and the newscast cuts away.

The next day, at school, my social studies teacher tells me he is sorry and asks if I have any family in Beijing. I say I don't, but the truth is I don't know. My cousins could be anywhere in China; I have never asked about those skinny preteens who played in that hotel bathtub, who would now be university age. My father would know, but he has been dead for nine months.

The Tiananmen Square protests trigger a formerly latent fear of Mao's brand of communism, and throughout the 1990s, waves of wealthy and middle-class immigrants from Hong Kong move to Canada, the United States, and Australia to proactively escape the looming 1997 handover of Hong Kong to Chinese governance. In Vancouver, the established Chinese community is filled with families just like mine, families who, after several generations, have learned to integrate into Canadian society by erasing their accents and living in unremarkable homes. We feel safe in our Vancouver Special, in a working-class neighbourhood of fading bungalows and backyard vegetable gardens, even if that sense of safety is a lie we tell ourselves. We have learned to survive by being boring and polite, apologetic and mundane. But the newcomers are something altogether different.

With their wealth, they have the means to start new lives in big suburban homes in subdivisions bordering golf courses with names like Westwood Plateau and Morgan Creek. Their children go to private schools—York House or Little Flower Academy or Vancouver College—institutions that more established Chinese families had never considered before, even if they could afford them.

In the end, the newer immigrants go on with their lives, unapologetically establishing their families in spacious homes in good neighbourhoods, relishing the relative freedom their children are growing up with.

The difference between the two communities—new and old—is noticed by everyone, not just us. On the news, a white homeowner complains about their newly arrived Chinese neighbour, who wants to cut down an old tree. Teens get arrested for street racing in luxury cars, their Chinese-ness always noted by the television reporters. The mugshots of young men who may or may not be members of Asian criminal gangs flash across our screens, their distinctly Chinese names—which, unlike mine, are not anglicized—marking each of them as a newcomer. The subtext is obvious: the recent Chinese immigrants are brash, disrespectful, and do not know their place.

At school, my grade nine English teacher opens a discussion about immigration and diversity, and several students voice their dislike of the changing Chinese community, repeating stereotypes about ugly stucco mansions and drug money. My face grows hot and I blurt out, "Not all Chinese people are annoying like that. My family has been here forever." But then I immediately feel shame for drawing a line between *us* and *them*.

"Oh, we don't mean people like you, Jen," they say. And my anxiety settles just a little. *Good*, I think, but then my stomach turns over on itself because I know that I have enacted a betrayal. My teacher does not admonish any of us and moves on to another topic. I slouch in my chair, exhausted.

♥

It's pathological, perhaps, to try to distill an entire culture into pithy explanations that foster comprehension across space and time, but it's a responsibility that was imposed on me—like the proverbial albatross—for as long as I can remember.

Are you related to Bruce Lee?

Why doesn't your mother learn English?

You don't sound Chinese.

♥

"This is the real crucible in East Asian representation, where it's like you are a Rorschach test for everybody. Everybody. Not even just Asian people. They will see what they want to see when they look at you, and they go, 'Hmm.' She had to make sure that she was holding on to some sense of self because everyone else in the world was trying to attach and hang certain things on her."

BOWEN YANG ON AWKWAFINA

"It's going to be hard to not walk into the room as an Asian American woman and not surprise someone with my bawdiness or the way that I yell. It proves a larger point that we're all different and come from different experiences, and just because this is how you see 'Asians,' that's not how I am. Let me be a little colour in your landscape."

AWKWAFINA

A few years ago, my friend Shane sent me a YouTube link with no explanation. "Watch this," he said. "I'm pretty sure you'll like it." That link led to the video and song that made rapper and actress Awkwafina famous, her ode to her own vagina, "My Vag."

The song is slacker rap, the kind of comedy song that is an evolution of "Weird Al" Yankovic, juggling juvenile potty humour with sharp pop culture subversion, and written and performed by an ostensible oddball. Awkwafina isn't styled; for most of the shoot, she's wearing a white T-shirt and black shorts and a giant pair of glasses. A bodyguard paints her nails. Improbable items shoot out from between a woman's legs—silly string, a whole head of cabbage, a can of soda—sometimes landing in Awkwafina's hands, sometimes hitting her in the face. I laughed, but I also wondered, *Who is she?*

At no point in this 2012 video does Awkwafina address the elephant in the room, which is how groundbreaking it was for a visibly Asian woman to perform a raunchy comedic song, have it go viral, and never once mention that she is Asian. The song is funny. Awkwafina is funny. Awkwafina is Asian. I imagined her shrugging while taking a hit off a bong, before saying, "So?"

When I was thirteen, I performed in a series of skits at my alternative high school's year-end drama show. In one, I played a surfer bro, obsessed with his swoop of perfectly waved hair. In another, I played a subverted version of the grandmother from Little Red Riding Hood. And finally, I performed an impression of Chuck Woolery, the ever-smiling host of the game show *Love Connection*. If the disconnect between who I truly was and who I was playing was visible to the audience, I didn't care. Whether they were laughing at my performance or the idea of someone like me attempting that performance, it didn't matter. I got the laugh, didn't I?

Nonchalance can be a pushback too.

♥

As a teenager, I did everything I could to appear less Chinese, which is a complicated thing to admit. Even though anyone could hear my Canadian accent as soon as I spoke—and I always spoke first and often, not only because I was an extrovert, but because I'd learned that doing so was useful in warding off questions about my origins—I was anxious to cement my identity as the girl who quit piano lessons, who cheated her way through Chinese-language school, and was not very good at math. I leaned hard into a grunge-rave-postpunk aesthetic, buying my second-hand jeans at Value Village, stacking my cassette collection of tortured indie bands in a place of honour on my bookshelf, reading and rereading books by white feminists who wrote about dystopias, English moors, the suffocating limits of small-town Canada. I learned to cook lasagna and crepes and vichyssoise. I dated white boys and Brown boys, but never Chinese boys. I walked, alone, from downtown to Stanley Park, where I followed the path beside the beach until I came to my favourite rock, the one that narrowed to a flat point into English Bay. If I sat there long enough, I could pretend my body—so anemic, so lactose intolerant, so flat-chested—no longer mattered. I was sunshine and salted air, warm rock and wet sand. It was always windy there. I loved the wind. It rendered my face numb with its sharp edges.

By the time I was nineteen, my transformation—from a nerdy Chinese girl who played the clarinet in the school band to the girl with the big pants and wallet chain who smoked weed between classes and danced at underground parties with white girls, glow sticks twisted in her hair—was complete. I stomped through the bookstore I worked at in steel-toed boots and read Seamus Heaney on the bus. I spoke Chinese only to my mother, and my vocabulary was shrinking by the day.

That summer, my mother asked me to attend a fundraising dinner for the Lee's Benevolent Association, a clan charity originally formed by the earliest Chinese immigrants to Canada. At the beginning of the twentieth century, Chinese men who shared last names formed groups to help support each other in their new country. They traded resources, helped with housing and jobs, planned parties to alleviate loneliness and depression. By 1995, the Lee association had been operating out of its own building for eighty-eight years. These dinners were important to my father and grandfather, a way of recalibrating, of remembering their pasts as uncertain young men in a country that had never wanted them. For my mother, it was an opportunity to talk to my father's friends, to remind her of his vitality, to take some sting out of his death.

At the restaurant on Fraser Street in East Vancouver, the banquet room was filled with men, mostly in their seventies or older, and a handful of women who were at least my mother's age. The men drank whisky (Johnnie Walker Red, of course), slapped each other on their backs, fumbled in their pockets for their packs of Player's Light. My mother and I, sipping at our tea, did not know all of these men, but they knew who we were. One after another they approached us, friends of my grandfather and father, and asked what my sisters and I were studying in school or doing for work, how my mother's health was. They dropped their voices to a whisper as they leaned in and said, "I'm sorry about your father and grandfather. They were good men."

For the first time, I realized my grandfather and father had both been young men when they came to this country, walking the streets of Vancouver with a straight posture that sometimes read as primness, even as they carried an unwieldy burden of otherness and fear. At nineteen, I walked those same streets with a slouch, dragging the hems of my oversized pants on the sidewalk. I never worried that I might be stopped on the street by police, that my presence could be construed as illegal. This relative freedom was what they had worked for, though they never experienced it themselves, and this filled me with an almost unbearable sadness.

I blinked and forced myself to look around the restaurant. Like my grandfather, the older men at this banquet wore pressed three-piece suits, stood with their hands clasped behind their backs. Like my father, the middle-aged men laughed loudly at off-colour jokes and shouted in a combination of Cantonese, Toisan, and English, the words all jumbled together.

An elderly man, quite possibly the oldest one in the room, sat down in an empty chair beside me.

"My dear," he said, "I hope you apply for the scholarship this year. You are Seid Quan's granddaughter. You must be a scholar too."

Not many people knew that my grandfather had always wanted to be an academic. After he had died, I had found a pile of his papers, yellowed and stiff, covered with neat vertical lines of calligraphy, painted with a traditional bamboo-handled brush and ink. My aunts had told us that he had learned to read English faster than any of his friends so that he could study the news and, later, be one of the first Chinese men to apply for citizenship when the Chinese Exclusion Act was struck down. My grandfather was a barber for most of his life, and he owned his own shop—the only one in Chinatown—but what he really wanted to do was read and study and give others a classical education. In the back of his shop, behind a half wall, he had built a small bed, narrower than a twin mattress, where he napped when the shop was empty. It seemed cruel that he had assembled a life with such small comforts, such brief reprieves, when the one thing he had always wanted, to teach and study, would never be a possibility.

"I'll for sure apply," I said. And the man shook my hand and walked away. I never asked how he knew my grandfather. And I never saw him again.

That weekend, I took the SkyTrain to the library downtown and found the shelf that held the books about the history of Vancouver's Chinese community. There, I found Paul Yee's *Saltwater City*, the seminal photographic history book that explores the roots of Vancouver's Chinatown and the lives of the people who lived and worked there. On the library's carpeted floor, I read about the first Chinese Canadian nurses, the first lawyers, the first members of parliament, the first Olympic athletes. But I also read about the men who died in the back country in the late 1800s, having been abandoned by the Canadian Pacific Railway and lacking the money to book a passage home. There were the children who were taunted by their white classmates, the interracial couples who hid their relationships, the women who worked in the sex trade, comforting the lonely men whose families remained in China, separated by the head tax and later the Chinese Exclusion Act. I took a pile of books home with me and read them quickly, more quickly than I had ever read *The Handmaid's Tale* or *Towards the Last Spike*.

Until then, I had not realized that being Chinese could mean *this* place, the city I was born in and had lived all my life. I had always imagined China and Canada as two separate bubbles, with me shuffling between the two, or more precisely, existing in a netherworld in between, a stateless place with no name and no markers. For my parents and grandparents, this disconnect was lived experience; they had migrated here, after all, and the definitions of *home* and *away* were constantly shifting, dependent on current events and how white people treated them. It must have felt like belonging was a myth.

But Vancouver's Chinatown, the twelve square blocks bordered by downtown on one side and industrial East Van on the other, could be mine. I knew those alleys by smell and sound, by the grid of power lines that crossed the sky above, the individual layouts of the produce piles outside each grocer. The puddles gleamed with leaked car oil, small rainbows floating on the surface of dirty water. So much beauty, but you had to look. You had to notice.

The people who had come before me had laid the foundation of this place, built the businesses, forged friendships that were as unshakeable as family, learned the systems of a country that had been designed to exclude them or treat them as units of labour. My father and grandfather had done all of that so that I could stand on Pender Street, looking up at the third-floor balconies, and feel that this was where I was meant to be.

♥

It's an amorphous state, being a Chinese Canadian author. I don't mean that I am ever confused by my cultural, national, and racial identities. What I mean is that as a person of colour in the public eye, and someone whose ideas and words are disseminated through books and social media, I'm often made painfully aware—through the questions I'm asked and the tweets I receive—of the public's confusion and assumptions about *me*, about my relationship with China, and about how at home I feel in Canada. Let's be honest: the book-buying public is overwhelmingly white. The publishing industry is overwhelmingly white. The book media is overwhelmingly white. And it was even more so when I went on my first book tour, to promote *The End of East* in 2007, when I was thirty years old.

Being the only person of colour in a room was nothing new to me. I was, for a year, the only Chinese student in my alternative arts high school. In my creative writing classes at university, there might have been two or three other racialized students in my year, but we were rarely in the same workshop. When I went out with my then-husband's friends, I was the only Chinese woman in the group, very often the only Chinese woman in the Irish pubs they frequented. In these spaces, I sometimes shrank and fell silent, or I sometimes puffed myself up and shouted about any topic presented to me, trying to assert my dominance before someone else could assert theirs first. Their dominance would, by extension, mean my submission.

Eventually, after people had grown comfortable with me, the questions or complaints or faux concern would start.

All the shops on Robson only carry Asian girl sizes.

Was Crouching Tiger, Hidden Dragon *really that good?*

How can we get the Chinese community more engaged in real culture?

What do you think of democracy in China?

What's a xiao long bao?

It became abundantly clear that they saw me as a tour guide. I was the friendly Chinese person who was Westernized and approachable enough to explain the mysteries of Chinese-ness in terms white people could understand. I wore jeans from the Gap, drank Caesars at brunch, and watched *Friends* every Thursday evening. What ended up happening, what I feel shame over even now, is that I didn't explain the real China to anyone, if such a thing is even possible. Instead, I told them what they wanted to hear, a China Lite that was easy to digest, didn't threaten anyone, and allowed us to carry on socially, cordial and at the edge of friendship.

I guess Asian women have the money right now.

I like it, but maybe that's only because I grew up on kung fu movies.

I'm Chinese and I love culture so I might be the wrong person to ask.

Yes, Tiananmen Square was a real shame.

It's a like a perogy.

♥

In Lulu Wang's film *The Farewell*, Awkwafina, in her first dramatic acting role, plays Billi, a failed American writer who travels to China to say goodbye to her dying grandmother, who hasn't been told that she has terminal cancer in an effort to keep her last days happy and peaceful. The family rushes to plan a wedding for Billi's cousin and his

Japanese girlfriend so that everyone can gather under the pretext of a celebration, rather than coming together to mark the end of a life. The film is a beautiful, touching tribute to the ways in which Chinese families strive to protect their elders, even if their methods are complicated, sometimes dishonest, and demand a cheeriness no one feels.

Throughout *The Farewell*, the language, food, and cultural touchstones of what it is to be Chinese are presented with a simple matter-of-factness.

Shortly after arriving at her grandmother's house, Billi sits down at the piano in the living room and begins playing a stormy, bombastic song, just as her father and uncle have settled in to drink whisky. As people argue behind her, Billi plays a musical accompaniment to her emotional turmoil, dressed in a baggy black T-shirt, a frown tightening her face. For Chinese North Americans, this scene raises the spectre of childhood piano lessons, the one instrument every Chinese family demanded their children learn to play. It didn't matter if you wanted to play bass in a rock band, as I did, it was always, always the piano. It's a symbol of intergenerational conflict, of the will of the family versus the will of the individual, of the eternal immigrant struggle for upward mobility.

But in this scene, that backstory and the significance of the piano for people of the Chinese diaspora is never explained. If you didn't know, you would experience Billi's tumultuous turn at the piano as an outlet for her grief in a moment where she is unable to speak it. The depth, the very Chinese-ness of this scene can be read on two levels, but Lulu Wang doesn't hold your hand through it. She simply presents it, and you can access it any way you like.

Later, we see that Billi's cousin, Hao Hao, played by Han Chen, is a hapless groom. Throughout the film, Hao Hao is silent, with no lines of dialogue, and expresses himself entirely through his body. He slouches, hangs his head, twists his mouth as if he is afraid he might cry. When Billi talks, he listens and places a hand on her shoulder, his floppy copper hair falling over one eye. He is, by far, my favourite character in the whole movie.

His silence is never explained, never addressed, never remarked upon. There is no discussion of how young men in Chinese families are often painfully shy, or how women often dominate their households and conversations, or how men rarely show emotion, their lives bordered by school, work, and stoicism. These points could have been raised, but they are not. Hao Hao is left to be himself, to let his silent jokes land as they need to. Does it matter if a non-Chinese audience might be confused?

When asked in an interview with *Harper's Bazaar* in 2021 about the expectations placed on Asian celebrities, Awkwafina said, "My whole life has been spent with people having an idea of what I'm about to be, where I come from, how I was raised. I've spent my entire life walking into a room surprising them." It seems fitting that Awkwafina, who first became famous for a comedy act not about race but about genitals, should perform her best work to date in a movie about the push and pull of familial expectations, where the viewer, if they are not Chinese, is left to fill in the cultural gaps.

♥

There is no doubt that Awkwafina's star has been rising for several years. From YouTube sensation to award-winning dramatic actor, to producer and star of her own sitcom, *Awkwafina Is Nora from*

Queens, she is, right now, a bankable performer, a destination celebrity. This, in and of itself, is a remarkable feat for an Asian woman in Hollywood, when for so long Asian performers were pushed to the side, playing restaurant servers or computer nerds, or relegated to dancing behind Gwen Stefani on her world tour.

In *Nora from Queens*, which first aired in 2020, Awkwafina plays an exaggerated version of herself from ten years ago. She is unemployed and lives with her father and grandmother in a small house in Queens. She falls asleep cuddling a very large purple vibrator. She tries to stage an ill-fated music festival. She moves to China to launch an app and spends much of her time trying to avoid an assistant who is far too devoted to her. She has a cousin who has a tail growing from the end of his spine. Her friends are misfits who sell coloured sand in glass bottles or are straight-laced seniors at the local private school.

In this not-quite-real New York, race is just a minor detail, not a mystery or a fetish or a teachable moment. People develop crushes, have disastrous haircuts, get fired from jobs that were never that good in the first place. The family might be Chinese—they look Chinese, eat Chinese food, even play with the stereotypes from vintage Chinese movies—but their Chinese-ness isn't asked to explain itself.

It was easy for me to see myself in Nora, but a version of myself who could be what she wanted and the world would just have to adjust. I wished my younger self had had this show. All this time, Awkwafina has been leading us here, to where *just being* is possible. It's the dream, isn't it?

But it's a dream that can come at a very high price.

For years, Awkwafina has been criticized for her use of African American Vernacular English, or what is often called a Blaccent, in projects that were specifically designed to be comedic and slapstick, in particular her breakout role as Peik Lin in the blockbuster movie *Crazy Rich Asians*. She addressed the criticism in 2022, on Twitter, in a statement that many, including me, found lacking. She didn't apologize for her cultural appropriation but instead reiterated that she never meant harm and that she will always uplift Black communities.

What she didn't say, and what I wished she would have said, is that white supremacy always seeks to divide racialized people, to pit communities against each other because if those groups united, the power would be unstoppable and white supremacy would topple. To that end, within the racial hierarchy established by white supremacy, there is a distinct function and place for each racialized community, and often Asian North Americans participate in reinforcing those roles. There is anti-Blackness in the Asian diaspora and there are no excuses for that, even though many of us are trying to do better.

Awkwafina grew up loving pop culture, especially hip-hop, and in those spaces, Asian women are all but invisible, even more so twenty years ago when Awkwafina was a child and forming her tastes. In the absence of role models in music or comedy that looked like her—or me—she turned to Black performers instead, which many racialized people who are not Black tend to do. For some people, connecting to whiteness is, quite frankly, undesirable, if not impossible. Instead, TLC or *The Fresh Prince of Bel-Air* or the films of John Singleton form a much closer and more direct relationship. This fandom can be joyful and imbued with layers of meaning, particularly in how racialized people can find points of kinship and reciprocity across communities that white supremacy would try to separate. Growing up in East Vancouver, where so few of the families were white, where the food and customs that were most familiar to us were never seen on television or in movies, my friends and I listened to Bell Biv DeVoe and watched *In Living Color* while laughing uproariously. The points of connection—imposed otherness, the drive for economic security, the alternating tensions of hypervisibility and invisibility—were deep and comforting. We weren't Black, but we felt the Black community could understand us.

The difference between Awkwafina and a regular, adoring fan is that she profited from her obsession with Black culture, and she made it the butt of jokes. This may have begun as fandom, but it grew ugly along the way. And she didn't acknowledge it.

If Awkwafina has brought us to a place where her race doesn't matter, it's at least partly because she first learned to move through and in between cultures, first as a fan and then as a misguided appropriator. She has, since *Crazy Rich Asians*, done some very good work, and she has the luxury now of looking back at her career and making amends for the exploitation she enacted to get her to this level of success. I don't know if she's doing this hard, self-examining labour, but I really, really hope she is. I want to believe that the learning she said she was committed to is real, but like her Blaccent, maybe it's all just a performance.

TWO

In 2017, a time when U.S. journalists were attempting to explain the xenophobia of the new Donald Trump administration, I was interviewed for National Public Radio's *Weekend Edition Saturday*. The episode focused on borders, and they were talking to Canadians who lived near the U.S. border, in cities like Vancouver, where the ebb and flow of culture can be fluid. In that interview, I talked about how Vancouver's location within the Asia Pacific region means the city plays an integral role in the movement of people, goods, and culture from countries like Korea and China. This international openness has had a significant impact—particularly in terms of diversity—on the ways in which Vancouver has developed.

Sometimes, when I am doing media, the conversations can get heated, especially if the themes of the book I'm promoting are emotionally charged. I have had to promote books that deal with sexual assault, racism, and refugees, and in those instances I expected some arguments to break out on Twitter or in the comments sections of various websites. But with this NPR interview, I walked away feeling just fine, believing I had said nothing controversial. Immigration, after all, isn't new, and neither is the Chinese diaspora.

The same day the interview aired, I received two emails, one vitriolically angry, the other sad and patronizing. Both writers disagreed that Chinese people had ever experienced racism at all and argued that we were lucky to have found homes in Canada and the United States, where the backward ways of our origins could be escaped. The angry email called me a "racist idiot" and claimed I must hate white people. The other explained, in a pleasant tone, that if I thought Canada was so bad, I should try living in China, where human rights are violated every day. It was a more articulate version of "go back to where you came from."

In the end, even my simple explanations of what it's like to be Chinese in North America were not simple enough. The thin ice of racism is so very, very brittle.

November 17, 2019

A new virus is discovered in Wuhan, China, possibly the result of animal-to-human transmission at a food market. As soon as I see the news, my heart sinks. My brain always knows when something will trigger a racist moment, as if my body is already bracing for impact. This sixth sense for potential racism may seem like an uncanny gift, but it's not. It's only survival, passed down from my parents and grandparents. And it's always right.

Once again, China is put under a microscope and the world begins to judge what Chinese people eat and how they treat their food, and question the hygiene and civility of a country that has struggled with density, urbanization, and astronomical middle-class growth. The lens has shifted, and we are looking at yet another version of China: a country that is a global leader in exporting goods, culture, and skilled workers, but whose citizens—the ones who make up the vast majority of its labour force in factories and farms—are still seen as the dirty, uneducated, backwoods folks the West has always suspected they were.

When I take my son to Chinatown to buy buns and walk through the Chinese garden, we see the racist graffiti on the walls of the cultural centre, on the stone lions flanking the gate on Pender Street. Or more specifically, I see it. My son walks by without even looking, without seeing the references to COVID-19 and the racial slurs I thought I would never see again. I decide not to point them out and let him enjoy the day, a pineapple bun in his hand. Even now, I am still not sure this was the wisest decision.

As people fall sick and die all over the world, anti-Asian hate crimes spike, the result of negative reactions to severe public health restrictions, fear, and just plain old racism. A seventy-one-year-old Chinese man is shot to death in Chicago's Chinatown. An elderly woman in San Francisco is punched in the head by a white man, but she fights back, beating him with a board she was carrying home for her garden. A finance executive is pushed in front of a New York subway train and dies.

Walking home from the pet food store, I pass by an apartment building, where a woman stands on a third-floor balcony. She yells racist slurs at me, waving her hands in rage. I say nothing and just keep moving, acutely aware that fighting back sometimes makes everything worse.

♥

As I write this, we are in the middle of a pandemic that has wreaked havoc for over two years. I am at home, with my son and my dog, trying to work as they bounce like mad electrons in circles through my small townhouse. COVID-19 is a pressing matter, one that has imposed on every aspect of our lives. There have been school closures. There have been times when we haven't been allowed to see friends, times when we were scared to buy groceries at a store, and times when the fear was immediate and everywhere.

I'm not a journalist. I don't write time-sensitive essays or try to make sense of current events. I watch, observe, and process for years before I am ready to write about anything that occurs, globally or personally. When I started writing *The Conjoined*, based heavily on my work in social services, I had not worked at a support agency in six years. When I wrote *The End of East*, my protagonist had just dropped out of her M.F.A. program, something I had done two years before I began writing her story. My writing brain is slow-moving, a snail that ignores the breathtakingly fast news cycle of refresh, read, and repeat. But this pandemic reaches far into the past, into what China has been, or at least how people who look like me have always been perceived in the West. And that is what I've been living with for the past forty-five years.

♥

Do Chinese people really eat bats?
Why do all the viruses come from China?
Does your mother eat weird wildlife?
Do you eat weird wildlife?
Do Chinese people really eat cats? Or dogs? Or snakes? Or bear paws?

♥

In *Saltwater City*, the book that changed the course of my intellectual and literary life, there is a reproduction of the December 1, 1921 cover of a publication called *The Anti-Asiatic Weekly*, which was published in Vancouver. The headline shouts, "An International Drug Plot." Throughout the early chapters of *Saltwater City*, Paul Yee cites multiple incidents of racism, almost all referencing the poor hygiene and low morals of Chinese men—men who are accused of raping white women, men who are assumed to be opium addicts, men who are vilified for living in a ghetto that breeds disease when the ghetto is the only place available to them. In 1924, a nursemaid named Janet Smith was found dead, and a Chinese houseboy, Wong Foon Sing, was suspected of her murder, despite the fact there was no evidence to support his guilt.

The fear of Chinese domination, often called Yellow Peril, isn't new. It's so old it predates highways, zipper flies on jeans, and hot water tanks in homes. For periods of time, the virulent racism sometimes fades, when the news focuses on another issue or when a Chinese person of note accomplishes something extraordinary. The resentment is then on a low simmer, relegated to whispered complaints about the upwardly mobile Chinese who travel the world in high style, or the visibly Asian teenagers who smoke and shout outside twenty-four-hour Vietnamese diners in the middle of the night. It can be the subtext in a newspaper article ostensibly about diversity and university enrolment, but specifically references the high numbers of Chinese students. Or it can be a little girl in my son's class, pulling her eyes back and chanting, "Ching chong ching."

But sometimes, when a new disease like SARS or H1N1 or COVID-19 emerges from one of China's densely populated cities, Yellow Peril erupts on a global level. Type "COVID" and "Chinese" into a search on Twitter and you will see. Racists pull out the most well-worn stereotypes imaginable. Chinese people will eat any part of any animal. We are dirty. We cough our mucous onto the street. We breed like rabbits because we are trying to take over the world. And on and on and on. The only difference between the old racist taunts and the new ones is the medium. Instead of mimeographed newsletters selling for ten cents, it's subthreads on Reddit, Instagram photographs of white teenagers dressing up as the coronavirus for a party, lengthy Facebook posts on why Chinese people should be shot on sight. But the content, predictably, remains the same. It's Yellow Peril all over again, except this time instead of the racist perceived threat of the lice-infested coolie with his buck teeth, thin pigtail, and his insatiable lust for white women and money, it's a real virus people are afraid of.

My reactions to this exhausting marginalization cycle between horror, rage, despair, and depression; these are predictable too. I will cry, shout at my phone, want to hide in my house for the rest of my life. Sometimes I think these reactions are ingrained, a kind of epigenetic generational trauma response that my cells remember—after all, my body contains DNA from a grandfather who travelled halfway across the world to start a new life in a country whose majority considered him inferior at best, a filthy contagion at worst. A recovering body takes on the remembered strength of its muscles. Maybe a traumatized body takes on the rage of its ancestors.

For me to write this essay now is less an act of timely journalism, and more an act of re-emerging activism. In my twenties, I might have put my head down and laughed along with the corona jokes, or tried to gently explain the proliferation of Yellow Peril stereotypes, all the while avoiding incendiary words and talking with a smile, so I could keep myself safe for just one more day, one more hour. But not now.

As a teen, I was a member of the Environmental Youth Alliance, a founder of my high school's Gender Equity Club. And still I stayed away from conversations or protests about race because it was too close, too much a part of my intimate knowledge. But I did learn how to shout, how to point out what's wrong and not take shit. Writing this now means dusting off those old skills and reapplying them to a topic that genuinely keeps me up at night, that used to make my grandfather so anxious that he kept every document referring to his immigration, financial, and health status, no matter how trivial or expired, in a cigarillo box in the top drawer of his dresser, so he could always prove he belonged. Nothing is new; everything is cyclical. Even racism and disease.

I once told an emerging writer—a racialized woman—that if she ever felt degraded by the systems and assumptions in the publishing industry, it would be over my dead body. I meant it. This essay is another way of shouting into the air. *Not on my watch.* Because maybe there are other aspiring writers who will read this, see me struggling to describe the most persistent fear of my existence, and think, *I can write into the hard things too.*

And yet I am so tired, so very tired, of this eternal loop, which I have never found a way to escape. It's a closed circuit and there is nowhere for us to go. But we have to try, right?

♥

One of the cousins I met in 1984, the little girl with the mosquito bites and jelly shoes, moved to Vancouver in 1996 and renamed herself Amber. At her wedding the next year, she wore a sequined red ballgown and was resplendently beautiful in a way that I could never have imagined when we were children. At her wedding, I sat with my mother, who pocketed the packs of cigarettes that were placed at every setting. "Just in case," she said, "one of your smoky uncles comes to visit."

I barely talked to Amber during those years, aware that she had created a new life for herself, with a husband who liked to show off his wealth with top-shelf Scotch and real shark fin soup. My mother and I were reminders of her poverty as a child, the lack she had fled.

In 2012, after years of little to no contact with her family, I met Amber and her teenaged daughter, Ruby, at a family dinner. Ruby told me she wanted to be a writer, and she wanted to know everything about publishing, about what kinds of things people liked to read and how hard it was for women of colour to break into the Canadian book industry. She spoke quietly but also very, very quickly, the words tumbling out of her mouth as if she couldn't control their launch into the air. Amber was then a single mother and tourism executive, calm and polished, a transformation of identity, if you will. The only thing I recognized in her was her wide smile, the kind that stretches so far and so genuinely, you feel compelled to smile in response.

"Remember when we met?" I asked her.

"Yes. I thought you were so stylish. So Canadian." Amber laughed. "I'm sure I seemed like a backward Mainland girl to you."

Yes, I wanted to say, *but also no*. I didn't understand her then, but it didn't matter. I was eight years old and had spent my entire life in Canada. I didn't have to understand her. I just had to accept her. She was my cousin, a little girl who kept her favourite shoes scrupulously clean and laughed in delight at the hot water rushing out of a tap.

After a moment, I said, "Your daughter reminds me of myself."

"Funny, right?" Amber shrugged. "She's so Canadian."

And it was true. Even if no one else ever thought so.

THE
PERFECT MOTHER

I am sitting in the front passenger seat of my family's copper-coloured station wagon, the car my father bought in 1980, when I was four years old. Out my window, I see Howe Sound and the small islands that rise like turtle shells from the blue, blue water. I look to my left and my mother is driving, big seventies-style sunglasses obscuring most of her face.

I yell over the wind roaring through the open windows. "Mom! When did you learn how to drive?"

She laughs and says, "I always knew how. I just didn't tell you, that's all."

The car takes a sharp turn on the highway and we tip, ever so slightly, toward the cliff that tumbles to the right. My mother thrusts her hand out the window and lets the wind lick at her skin. "Isn't this fun?"

I am scared shitless. I see another tight turn ahead. At the speed we're going, we'll never make it, but I can't look away. I place my hands on the dashboard and brace myself, and my stomach turns over on itself before I wake up.

♥

I have been having this recurring dream for as long as I can remember. Sometimes I call it a nightmare, although it's not nearly as frightening as the terrors I experienced in my childhood, when I would scream so loudly in the middle of the night my sister Penny would wake me by holding my shoulders and shaking me or, once, by punching me in the chest. In one dream, a group of faceless men drags my sister Daisy away from us as she kicks and screams. The last I see of her is her shoes being pulled through a doorway. In another, a gorilla chases me around my elementary school playground, his steps pounding louder and louder as he gains on me. I open my eyes just as I feel his hot breath on the back of my neck.

This dream of my mother though—where she is so clearly not herself, where she is no longer afraid of driving or water or cliffs, where she finds pleasure in feeling the wind on her skin—is the one that has lingered long into my adulthood, because this version of my mother is clearly an unfulfilled fantasy, a wish twisted by my sleeping self. She has never driven a car, never appeared to have a good time in my presence, never laughed with ease. Daily life is something to survive, never something to savour. So the dream is an upside-down nightmare or, rather, a surprising dreamscape of joy until the very end, when the nightmare asserts itself and I realize that, just as in real life, I don't trust my mother.

♥

Motherhood, as it's presented to us in pop culture, is simultaneously an exercise in visibility and invisibility. When I was a child, television was the nexus of what I understood culture to be, and from a very young age, I was aware that those mothers I saw on TV were symbols of admonishment. Watching them reminded me that my mother, with her extreme sadness and rage, was not normal. With her unruffled pageboy hair, Elyse on *Family Ties* smoothed over her family's disagreements, her gaze always loving, always softly checking on her four children, rather than hawkishly tracking and remembering their mistakes for future tirades. Clair on *The Cosby Show* pushed her children to be the very best versions of themselves with nothing more than the occasional rise of a stern eyebrow, rather than shouting a litany of their flaws while furiously cooking dinner. Maggie on *Growing Pains* was a tall calm ballast while her children swirled around her, not a chaotic tornado that tore through the house, shedding rage in every room. Despite their perfection—all three women were also thriving professionals, with Elyse working as an architect, Clair as a lawyer, and Maggie as a journalist—I never wished for any of these women to be my mother, but I watched them with a precise, obsessive focus: how they tried to never hurt their children's feelings, how they genuinely liked their family's company, how they knew what each of their children liked or hated or was good at.

When I think about these women now, they were visible, sure. But they were only visible in relation to their families. If they wept in their beds at night because their individual identities were slipping away, or if they had affairs with a new co-worker to make them feel alive again, we never knew. Who they once were, or who they still could be, had been obliterated, made invisible by a proven sitcom formula, by the world's expectations of how mothers could, or should, fade into the background.

♥

Things my mother has told me about her life as a young woman in Hong Kong:

She sang in a girl group with two friends. Her favourite number was a cover of "Que Sera Sera," as performed by Doris Day.

She had a boyfriend who wanted to marry her, but she thought his ass was too big.

She dropped out of high school one year before graduation.

She loved her mother, her home, and trying on dresses with her sisters in their room.

Her dream was to sing onstage for a living, an audience holding their breath as they listened to her soprano voice rise through a concert hall, notes hovering in the air. The people in the crowd would have heard her, they would have seen her, and this affirmation is what would have lifted her voice even higher.

What actually happened is that, at nineteen, my mother stopped singing in public to sail to Canada to marry my father. By twenty, she was pregnant with her first child, and over the next eighteen years, she would have four more children, her body growing softer and wider with every pregnancy. All the things she loved—swimming, big band music, eating at fancy restaurants—fell away as she was tasked with ushering her daughters into successful lives, as if her own didn't matter anymore, as if it was too late for her to even try. If she sang "White Christmas" in her heavily accented English, her daughters— now her only audience—squirmed. With limited English and little Canadian work experience, she watched as she was whittled away, layer by invisible layer, until the only part that was left was her hard, immovable, fiery hot anger. Eventually, she found herself sitting in crowds of thousands at five university graduation ceremonies, where even the sound of her clapping was engulfed by the echoing applause. By then, she wouldn't have sung a note, even if we'd asked her.

♥

In 2000, I was twenty-three years old and engaged to be married, the first of my friends to be planning a wedding. I was officially on an academic leave from my creative writing M.F.A. program, but I had no plans to return, citing the program's inability to meet the needs of racialized and working-class students, and the isolation of living in Montreal, where I felt badly out of place and my tiny studio apartment's only window looked out at the brick wall of the neighbouring building ten feet away. I had, like most aspiring writers, dreamed of becoming a member of the local literary scene, even if what I envisioned—champagne, knowing chuckles over jokes about Jacques Derrida—was far from what CanLit had ever really looked like. But I would have settled for a group of friends, for instructors who nurtured idiosyncrasies in their students, rather than treating them all is if they were the same. Every time the class discussion turned to theory or Don DeLillo, I couldn't help but think the program was designed for wealthy white boys whose parents were paying the bill without even asking what kind of career this might lead to. When no one spoke to me at the student open mics or as we waited for our professors to arrive in classrooms, I shrank and fell silent. I'm sure no one in my program even noticed.

What I didn't tell anyone was that I had been drowning in the first major episode of depression of my young life. If I didn't need to be in class, I was in bed weeping, my brain circling over the painful moments of my childhood, how my poems had been harshly criticized in class, how much I missed my boyfriend back home. I slept twelve to fourteen hours every night. I rarely ate and became so thin that my periods grew sporadic and the hair on my temples began to fall out. After one term, unsure of what else to do or who to ask for help, I sold all of my furniture, packed my clothes and books, and flew home.

My boyfriend picked me up from the airport and dropped me off at my mother's house. I remember letting myself in with my key, walking through the empty ground floor where my sisters once slept, and dropping my bags in my old room, with its magpie collection of posters—*Swingers*, Picasso's *Blue Nude, Three Men and a Baby*. I took a deep breath and slowly approached the kitchen, where my mother was making fried noodles for lunch. She turned her head to look at me but didn't stop cooking. When she reached out her hand, I handed her the sesame oil without her even asking.

"You're back," she said. I could hear no emotion in her voice as she peered into the wok, her glasses fogging up from the steam. She didn't hug me and I felt deflated, even though I'd known an embrace was unlikely; it had been years since she had touched me. Then she added, "I knew you weren't good enough."

And then we sat down at the table and ate, as we always had. My mother ate her noodles calmly and I followed her lead, leaning back into the green vinyl chair I had been sitting in since I was five. It was too small and the cracked seat cover scratched at the backs of my thighs. I didn't fit, but I was well used to that.

My friends and I returned to the same dance clubs we'd always gone to and drank double gin and tonics as usual while the nights ebbed away to relentless basslines that never seemed to change. In the daytime, I babysat my nephew, who welcomed me back to Vancouver with a handmade card and a tight, sweaty hug. Everything was back to normal. I almost forgot I had ever been away.

A year later, I was working three jobs, trying on wedding dresses, and still not writing. In rare quiet moments, I could write only fragments about Montreal, about my boots on the cold sidewalks, the neon lights of the strip clubs, the limestone saints on spires. Those lines floated in my head, not quite poems, not even complete thoughts. I wrote them down, crossed out words that weren't working, doodled, then closed my notebook. I had never before been unable to write; my life had been marked by loss and worry and fear, but I had always used writing to keep myself afloat, to organize the tumble of my emotions.

After a few months, I began to see those poetic fragments as traces of my depression, something I needed to bury beneath a hum of activity. Writing, instead of being a retreat or a balm, was dismantling all the work I had done to cover my sadness with a brittle veneer of functionality. So I met with four different wedding florists instead. I bought fancy white heels. I cried late at night, when no one else was awake.

That summer, on a warm evening in August, my sister Daisy and I were trying to help my mother make dinner. Daisy had come back to Vancouver from Singapore for my wedding with her two small children, Jacob and Bridget, both of whom spoke with unsettling and hilarious Singaporean-British-Canadian accents, making them seem like very tiny adult expats. By then, my mother and I had not been in a fight for many years. After the death of my father, she had barely noticed me and kept to herself, leaving me to navigate my way through high school and university on my own. But since I'd returned from Montreal, I noticed that she had been slowly coming back to life. She began cooking elaborate dinners again, going to the Richmond Night Market with her friends, and travelling by bus to the casino just across the border. She laughed at my fiancé's jokes, most of which she could only partially understand. She was softer, as if having finally emerged from her grief, she was figuring out who she was in this new life without a husband, her children all grown, and her youngest daughter engaged to be married to a lawyer. There was so little to worry about, so little to rage at.

But that evening, my mother, a cleaver in one hand and a long pair of cooking chopsticks in the other, was in a rage. She was rushing from stove to sink to fridge and back again, and there was nothing Daisy and I could do right. She yelled old criticisms at us, phrases I hadn't heard since I was twelve years old.

"So useless. Your boyfriend will never marry you."

"That's the dark soy. I need light soy! Stupid girl."

"I gave birth to five daughters and not one of you was worth the labour."

After a half hour, I stopped trying to look cheerful and instead stomped through the tasks she assigned with a scowl on my face. I slammed bottles of oyster sauce and Maggi seasoning on the counter, and I rolled my eyes when my mother complained. When Daisy's children called her away, I could see relief etched on every part of her body as she left the kitchen.

I made yet another supposed mistake, and my mother growled at me, "Everyone else's daughters can cook and clean and act like they respect their mothers. Not you. Ungrateful, useless idiot."

I whirled around, my hands in fists. "Would it kill you to say, just once, 'Thank you for helping me, Jen'?"

She stopped tossing the vegetables in the hot wok. "What did you say to me?"

"Maybe you could thank us or show us you love us once in a while," I said, straightening up, my spine at attention. I was half a head taller than my mother and she was forced to tilt her head up to look into my eyes.

"For what? For being the worst daughters I have ever heard of? For making me embarrassed every day because you can't do anything properly? For thinking you're better than me just because you all went to university and speak perfect English? Why should I thank you for being useless?"

My own rage was building, and I could feel my eyes burning with tears that I tried to blink back. In that moment, I remembered every time she had failed me. Her absence at parent-teacher meetings. Her derisive laughter when she saw me waiting by the phone for a boy to call. Her footsteps when she angrily paced the house, looking for me, as I hid under the dining room table. If she found me, she would berate me, maybe about the hair in the drain or the mud I had tracked in or the spider I had let spin a web in my room.

I could hit her, I thought, *I want to hit her*.

Instead, I raised my voice, something my sisters and I rarely did, and shouted, "You don't love me! All I ever wanted was for you to love me. You have never said you loved any of us."

Before I could say another word, my mother slapped me, once on the right cheek, and then again on the left. "How dare you," she hissed. "You need to learn your place."

"Hit me again," I whispered. "You can't hurt me."

I was barely aware of the tears rolling down my face, or Daisy's presence beside me. When I looked up, my niece and nephew, then four and six years old, were standing at the door to the hallway, huddled together. Daisy touched my arm.

"It's not worth it," she said quietly. "She'll never understand."

My mother pushed past the children and rushed to her bedroom. I heard the door slam and the springs in her mattress groan.

"But she needs to know," I said, my words tumbling out. "She never says she loves us. She isn't a real mother!"

"I know, Jenny. I really do. We've all had this fight with her before. Trust me: she'll never change. It doesn't matter how much you yell at her." She placed her fingertips on my cheek. "It'll be okay. The redness will go away." And then she turned to her children, took their small hands in hers, and led them away, so I could cry in private.

♥

The world is divided into two types of people: those who abhor the dominance that the Kardashian-Jenner family holds over the media landscape, and those who gleefully participate by watching reruns of their long-running reality television show, *Keeping Up with the Kardashians*. It can be impossible to predict which camp someone falls into. Some people applaud the Kardashians for succeeding in the intersecting industries of fashion, lifestyle, and television, which can exploit and marginalize women, particularly women of colour. Others hate their obsession with the accumulation of wealth and regard them as the very worst examples of late-stage capitalism, where money and fame, no matter how they are earned, are the ultimate prize. You either love the staged (and sponsored) Instagram photos in which everyone's outfit matches the luxury sports car, or you hate them, picking apart the notoriously Photoshopped thigh gaps and hair extensions. Their homogeneity in fashion and business—toned glutes, tight leather dresses, self-referential brands—either seems like a cute family similarity, or a sinister Stepford sister construction built to make money hand over fist.

But there can be little debate, however, that the Kardashian-Jenners have made visibility a commodity, monetizing their stranglehold on television, social media, and celebrity magazines. There are no shadows to retreat into for sisters Kourtney, Kim, Khloé, Kendall, and Kylie, only a spotlight of hypervisibility that is impossible to ignore.

See, the thing is, I *like* the Kardashians.

I'm not someone who expects perfection in my celebrities; in fact, I much prefer the opposite. I want to see the acne breakouts, hear them discuss their mental health struggles on *Red Table Talk*, see them stumble through a workout. The Kardashians, at first glance, are the antithesis of this, their appearances on red carpets and editorials so perfect as to render them robotic. And yet there is still a messiness to their lives, or at least the lives they allow the public to see—a messiness I love.

It began in 2007, when eldest sister Kim Kardashian, then known as the pretty assistant to Paris Hilton who appeared sporadically on

Paris's reality show, *The Simple Life*, shot into tabloid notoriety when a sex tape with a former boyfriend was released online. Celebrity sex tapes were nothing new even then, but Kim's was polished and well lit, her makeup and lingerie carefully put together. The fact remained, however, that her quick ascent was incited by a sex tape that had gone public. (No one has ever been able to figure out who was behind the leak). So Kim's fame has its roots in a kind of chaos, an intimate moment gone viral, a phenomenon that couldn't have been predicted. For someone like me, who has always loved the break in Rihanna's voice and the fatigue in Amy Winehouse's eyes, this flawed and chaotic humanity was exactly what I sought out in celebrity culture. And it was precisely this impulse that led me to keep track of Kim as she started to appear on gossip sites like *Perez Hilton* and *Page Six*.

Notoriety from sex tapes can fade overnight, but people soon learned that her father, Robert Kardashian, had been one of O.J. Simpson's defence attorneys during his infamous murder trial, and that Kim belonged to the same wealthy, fame-hungry crowd as Paris, Nicole Richie, and Lindsay Lohan, young women who had ridden the waves of their public scandals and misbehaviours to score acting jobs, launch clothing lines, and date billionaire shipping heirs or rock stars. Someone was going to see the business potential in Kim. As it turns out, it was her own mother.

♥

Things my mother said to me after my divorce:
"No one else will ever want you now."

"You are ruining my grandson."

"You were always the uncontrollable one."

"Your ex-husband's new wife is very pretty. I can see why he chose her over you."

"Stepfathers will molest your child."

"I am so ashamed."

♥

"The Devil works but Kris Jenner works harder."
@JNAJEFFERSON

My mother has five daughters. Kris Jenner has five daughters. Like many mothers with large families, my mother and Kris have always been obsessed with survival, with equipping their children with the tools and the will to become self-sufficient as quickly as possible. There is often no safety net in a large family, only a mother's divided attention, which never seems quite enough. For large families made up primarily of daughters, this focus on survival is doubly acute; not only is it about ensuring financial and professional stability, it's also about personal safety. Girls get assaulted. Girls get abused. Girls can disappear without a trace.

Some mothers would have tried to bury the sex tape. Some would have wanted revenge for their daughter's exploitation. Some would have raged at their daughters for making that tape in the first place. Some would despair for the future. Not Kris. When Kim's sex tape became so hugely popular that it was renamed *Kim Kardashian: Superstar*, Kris saw an opportunity: Kim was the perfect hook to lure viewers into a reality TV show, but the rest of the family—Kris's five daughters; her son, Rob; and her then-spouse, former Olympian Caitlyn Jenner—would keep the audience enthralled.

From the very beginning, the show was an endearing jumble. The Kardashian-Jenners were a large, bustling, somewhat tacky family living in the affluent suburb of Calabasas, California, where it seemed to always be summer and where everyone drove luxury cars in the blistering sunshine. Older daughters Kourtney, Kim, and Khloé spoke in a California doll-like drawl and seemed to have very little to do other than dress mannequins at their clothing store. Caitlyn shouted at the two youngest, Kendall and Kylie, who never listened. Kris jumped from one parenting disaster to the next, with an unflagging cheerfulness that rarely cracked under stress. In retrospect, it's easy to see that the exposure of her family's heartbreaks and foibles was purposeful. Her game was a long one. And its foundation was visibility, no matter the visibility's origins.

Kris can appear Machiavellian, Svengali-like, or, more benignly, like Professor Henry Higgins in *Pygmalion*. Kris could also be called an alchemist for seeing the earning potential in her children, but there is something else at play. Kris *sees* her children. She knows exactly what they can and can't do, what they can and can't sell. She knows they can't sing or dance or act. She knows that fame was never abhorrent to them. And she has turned who they are into a money-making machine.

I could never imagine my mother seeing me this way, or seeing me much at all. And, as if I was re-educating myself by leaning into a different hard maternal extreme, I could not stop watching.

♥

Things I found in my mother's room while snooping:

Every birthday card and Mother's Day card I ever made, in the trash.

A drawer full of unopened makeup and hand cream and perfumes, all gifts from my sisters and me.

A romance novel, in Chinese, dog-eared and faded, water stains on its cover.

The first book I wrote, illustrated and bound, and left with her for safekeeping, in the trash.

That's when I stopped snooping.

♥

Make no mistake: Kris Jenner likes fame too. Through her children, she grew famous because of proximity, but also because she played the reality show business better than anyone else before or since. She loves excess, wearing Balmain and Versace. On television, Kris was entertaining: willing to get drunk on winery tours with her daughters, allowing the cameras to capture her plastic surgeries and facial injection mishaps, dropping pithy quotes like, "If somebody says no, you're talking to the wrong person." She's giggled on camera about her fulfilling sex life, her lipstick smeared over her cheek. In the beginning, Kris was fame-adjacent, a business coach, a mom who could draw up a budget. By the time *KUWTK* finished its run in 2021, she had jumped all the way in, her enthusiasm for all the material benefits of fame eternally motivating. The family business plan, which has always been based on cross-platform omnipresence, was continuing to work beautifully.

Kris is the opposite of the sitcom mothers I watched in the 1980s. Just like them, she lives vicariously through her children, but she has her own persona to manage too, one that is overbearing, emotionally engaged, and relentlessly capitalist. She doesn't disappear into her children; rather, she has moulded her children to meet a specific, wealth-obsessed standard, and she emerges from their success with her own ring light, her own meme-able behaviour, in a five-thousand-dollar sequinned pantsuit, flush with the ten per cent manager's commission she makes on their income.

She is the opposite of my own mother too, because of her minute interest, her loving posts to her daughters on Instagram, the pervasive feeling that the lives of her children have provided fuel for her own reignition. My mother did her job as she faded away. Long into her children's adulthoods, Kris continues to assert her presence at every possible moment and, for me anyway, the resulting jumble—uncomfortable, flashy, and melodramatic—is destination viewing.

It really does seem that Kris works harder than anyone, even the Devil.

♥

This essay is a roller coaster of guilt. I love my mother, but my love for her is a complicated beast, one that has shaped every relationship in my life, usually for the worse. Like her, I have a quick temper. Like her, I have been felled by depression. Like her, I felt myself disappearing after my son was born; I stayed in bed for as long as I could and cried when I was awake. Like her, I have blamed others for all of my mistakes. Ask any of my partners, former or current. They could tell you.

Unlike her, I could never be invisible. Or quiet. My laugh is too big, my voice too loud, my desire to be seen too explosive. "Change your clothes," she would say. "You're showing too much cleavage." And she would turn away, as if my body was an insult, a test of manners that I was never able to pass.

I try to be grateful for what she gave my sisters and me. My mother fed and clothed us, kept a clean house, and saved all the money she could so we could go to school and take piano lessons and walk into the wide world with ease, confident with education and language and ability. When I launched my third novel, I remember standing under the spotlights on a stage where everyone could see me, even my mother, who watched from her seat at the back, her small body hidden from the crowd. She sat beside the book table, silent, counting the copies I sold, smiling wordlessly at the bookseller, listening to the conversations in English around her about books she could never read.

In the beginning, the invisibility was forced upon her. Later, she retreated into it. It was what she knew, the only space that felt designed just for her.

♥

If you want, you can find my favourite Kris moment on YouTube, a clip of her saying, with a wide smile on her face but an edge to her voice, "Never go against the family."

♥

In 2007, when my first book was published, my mother called, shouting at me through her phone. "Your book is at Costco! There are seventy-two copies! I counted them all!"

Every week for the next three months, my mother called me from Costco to tell me how many copies were left until they sold out. "They're gone! All gone! How much money did you make?"

This is the story I tell whenever someone at a book event asks if my mother is proud of my success, if I don't want to peel back the layers of disappointment and resentment and hurt. It's the kind of cute story one might tell about a stage mother, a still-unformed Kris Jenner. But there is more to unpack. There is ambition, both my mother's and mine. There is the reality of the industry that I work in, the book industry, which has traditionally excluded women like my mother who hover on the edges of literacy, whose engagement in majority culture is limited by language and isolation. I write the books. My mother counts them at Costco. The gulf between those two acts is vast.

My sisters' jobs are as follows: business administration professor, counselling psychologist, owner and chief financial officer of an urban interiors store, communications and marketing director. My mother watched us as, one by one, we walked out of the house and claimed our spaces in the world, whether it was the first day of kindergarten or university graduation. She watched us button up our first business suits, pack our first briefcases, smooth down our hair on our way to jobs in real offices, where we were deemed capable. She watched us go, which meant she was always the one left behind.

How angry that must have made her. How much she must have hated us.

♥

On the spectrum of motherhood, Kris Jenner represents a complete integration of parent and child, the kind of mother who doesn't know her children have boundaries, who could bound into any of their homes and know exactly where they keep the hand towels, the olive oil, the sunscreen. I imagine she has her children's bank account numbers memorized. During those twenty seasons of *KUWTK*, I watched Kris defend, scold, encourage, and turn her children into business assets. She has negotiated their product endorsements, fashion collaborations, spinoff reality shows, and paid nightclub appearances. She has protected them from cheating partners, invasive media, and unfavourable professional contracts. She has helped them build businesses, fold businesses, marry partners who could become a part of the family business, and weather divorces. Her life, in the context of the show anyway, is centred almost entirely on her children. Her children are her business.

In one clip, Kris takes a call from Kendall, who is in the middle of an anxiety attack, and cuts short a business meeting to rush her to the hospital. Kim, watching it all unfold, calmly explains to those assembled in the boardroom, "Every day, a kid has an emergency." For several years, Kris has protected Rob, her only son, from the public eye, giving him space and time to manage his depression, single fatherhood, and a difficult relationship with body acceptance. For many, watching *KUWTK* is easy, a kind of escapism when our busy brains need a break, even when a member of the family is struggling or experiencing emotional upheaval. But for me, it's not quite that. Kris's hyperattention can be funny or absurd, but it also puts a glaring spotlight on the fact that parental love, or the fierce facsimile of it, is something I never knew was possible when I was a child. Several days could pass without my mother asking me a single question about school or my friends or the stories I was writing. It wasn't until my adolescence, when my sisters began moving out of the family home, that I understood there were other ways of mothering. I had been watching it on television my entire life.

♥

In pop culture, mothers can be mean and cold, like Betty Draper in *Mad Men*, or they can be sweet and kind and nurturing, like Elyse, Clair, and Maggie from the family sitcoms of my youth. But very few mothers in the public eye before Kris Jenner have been so deeply involved with their children, emotionally and financially; so much so that watching their show can be a shitstorm of discomfort. In one early episode, Kris goes to pole-dancing class with Kim, undulating in five-inch heels while Kim looks on, mortified. In another, she gulps down tequila shots until Khloé shouts at the bartender, "She needs to be cut off!" Nothing her children do is beyond her purview.

It's hard for me to watch *KUWTK* without remembering that my own mother has never asked about my anxiety disorder, taken me prom dress shopping, or known my shoe size. She is the kind of mother who has never known the names of my closest friends, who only comes to visit when my son has a birthday, who stopped going to my book launch parties because they all seemed the same to her. She would never manage my invoices. She would never want a key to my house. If I went missing, it would take her weeks to notice.

Like all extreme opposites though, Kris and my mother are, at their core, the same.

When children leave, when they grow up, when they try and fail, or try and succeed, a mother can accompany them, hoarding the energy they glean from the hum of activity. Or a mother can stay behind in their old homes, now empty, save for the echoes. Kris Jenner needed the energy, needed to be seen. My mother needed that once too, when she sang for an audience at sixteen years old. But she became caught in her isolation, hidden by years of not knowing how she could ever enter the world again. And rather than try and risk failure, she retreated.

♥

When I was pregnant, I wrote my son a letter that I can't find now, after two moves and a divorce. I remember I read it out loud when it was finished and I cried a little, because I knew I would miss the feeling of carrying him with me everywhere I went, that constant double personhood. He would soon be an individual separate from me, in a body that was entirely his own, and this seemed like another profound loss. After a series of losses from my childhood onward, I dreaded this one with a sharpness that grew in intensity the closer we got to my due date.

In the letter, I wrote about my family, about his father's family, about the many people waiting to meet him. I wrote that I hoped he would be kind and empathetic and would try to make the world a better place. But I also wrote that he would have his own ambitions, his own favourite foods, his own relationships with people he loved or hated or both. And I promised I would try not to change him into the child I wished he could be, but rather help him be the best version of the person he already was.

I have broken a lot of promises since then, but not that one.

My son is emotional, creative, independently minded, logical, and a smug know-it-all. He cracks good jokes. He is writing a novel. He cheats at board games. He likes his hair to fall over his right eye. His body is always warm, always ready to break into a run so he can feel the wind wicking the sweat from his skin. I sometimes wish he could control his feelings.

When I watch him cry or rage or hug himself, it hurts me too, in this body where he and I were once the same being. In those moments, if I could take away this one very tender part of himself, I would. But this is a change that would not make him better or safer or more successful; this would be a change for me, his mother, who is someone who also burns out from sadness or anger or frustration and hates it. Instead, I watch him ride these emotions, and when he is done, I soothe and comfort and manage. He is exactly who he is meant to be and I am simply holding him until he is ready to launch himself— visibly or otherwise—into the outside world.

♥

Recently, my sisters and I rented a townhouse in Whistler, where we stayed for a long weekend with our mother and children. During that time, my mother told my sister Penny that she should never have broken up with her ex-boyfriend from twenty years ago, before concluding that he was too handsome for our family anyway. She tried to plan the details of her funeral over tea. She addressed my son by calling out "baby boy" in Chinese, and it made me question if she has ever learned his name.

One evening, after my mother had gone to bed, my sisters and I drank tea and wine and the conversation, as it often does, turned to our childhoods. Our mother, in her bedroom under a quilt, had no idea we talked about her rages, the ways in which she compared us to other children, how the only grief that mattered to her in the years after my father's death was her own. Once, when I was thirteen, I told her that I missed my father. She replied, "I lost a husband. You only lost a father. What are you crying for?" And then she walked away.

My nieces listened to our stories, fascinated but also confused. In their experience, their grandmother was generous and silly, handing out tubes of Pringles and fifty-dollar bills to the grandchildren, trolling the Safeway aisles after Halloween for discount candy that she would press into their hands at every visit. We turned to the girls and said, "She's a good Poh Poh. She's always been nice to you." And it was true, even if she often couldn't tell the kids apart.

What we didn't say is that it's a very specific grief to realize that your mother has saved the very best versions of herself for someone else, even if that person is your own child. There were many factors that contributed to my mother's rages and silences—isolation, depression, otherness, systemic racism, and misogyny—but still. All along, she might have been capable of kindness and affection and generosity, but she was too wrapped up in her own cocoon to access any of it. Perhaps she grew mellow with age, as many people do. Or perhaps she felt freer with her grandchildren because she could love them without bearing any responsibility for raising them. Or perhaps she understood that her daughters had never truly enjoyed her company, and this was a pattern she did not want to repeat. None or all of this could be true. But we grieved anyway.

♥

Whenever I try to think of a famous mother whose relationship with her children is something I could emulate, I draw a blank. There are, of course, admirable mothers in the world, women like Michelle Obama or Angelina Jolie or even soft-voiced Peg in *Edward Scissorhands*, as played by Dianne Wiest. But I have a difficult time focusing on the kind of mother I could be, or what I want, because I am too busy defining myself by what I shouldn't be.

It's easier, it seems, to look at the extremes—Kris Jenner and my mother—and be relieved that I'm managing to *not be them*. I have not turned my son into his own brand or started an Instagram account so he could attract sponsorships. I have never screamed that he is useless or demanded an apology when he has done nothing wrong. But between those two polarities, there exist a million ways to mother your children, and as many choices to be made that could result in multiple outcomes. Maybe this is the work that I have to do: envision a lifetime of motherhood that I alone get to define, and that isn't shaped by the missing pieces of affection and validation that characterized my childhood. I know what not to be. But I'm not sure what I could be.

Maybe my mother hadn't known either.

♥

The cover of my first novel features a Chinese woman in profile, sitting with a cup of tea. When I first handed my mother her copy, she held it in her hands, turned it over, running her fingers over the smooth coated paper. She didn't need to be able to read English to know that the book was very *Chinese*. She gazed at my author photo on the back. She nodded, as if to say, *Yes, that's my girl*.

"What do you write?" she asked me. "What is in the book?"

"Stories," I said. "About Chinatown. About families."

Her face lit up. "About me?"

"Not really. There is a mother in my stories though."

"Oh." The disappointment seemed to wash over her and she sighed. "I hope you are kind to her."

ACKNOWLEDGMENTS

To Anita Chong and the entire team at McClelland & Stewart, for believing a weird book about why I love pop culture deserves to be out in the world.

To Carolyn Swayze and Samantha Haywood, for always trusting my creativity and abilities, even when I did not.

To my family and friends who appear throughout this book, for being my best companions in life, in writing, in everything.

To my writerly friends—Dina Del Bucchia, Andrea MacPherson, Amber Dawn, Carrie Mac, David Ly, and everyone else I have had the privilege to cry and laugh with—who listened to me complain, who read portions of this book, who helped me manage the business of writing.

To the British Columbia Arts Council and the Canada Council for the Arts, for their financial support in the development of this book.

To Oscar, Jeff, and Rosie, my greatest loves. None of this is worth it without you.

A previous version of "The Orphan" was published as "What Anne of Green Gables Taught Me about Grief" in *The Walrus* in May 2019.

A previous version of "The Good Princess" was published as "The good princess: What Diana taught me" in the *Globe and Mail* in May 2018.

NOTES

THE ARTIST

The Bob Ross quote ("I was the guy . . .") is from the article "Bob Ross Uses His Brush to Spread Paint and Joy" by Linda Shrieves, *Orlando Sentinel*, July 6, 1990.

THE PERFECT PRINCESS

The Diana quotes ("You've got everything . . ."; "I would like a monarchy . . .") are from the 1995 television interview with Martin Bashir for BBC's *Panorama*.

THE BOYS ON FILM

The lines of verse beginning "he watches you . . ." are from "What We Do in the Name of Money" by Evelyn Lau, *You Are Not Who You Claim* (1990).

The lines of verse beginning "O in my dreams . . ." are from "Lawyer" by Evelyn Lau, *You Are Not Who You Claim* (1990).

THE BAD GIRL

Margaret Cho's comment to Kore Asian Media is quoted in the article "The 14 Women Who Changed Television," *The Telegraph*, May 10, 2017.

Amy Tan's comment ("I'm freed . . .") was made during Tan's television appearance on *George Stroumboulopoulos Tonight*, December 4, 2013.

THE COUGAR

The magazine profile of Gwyneth Paltrow referenced is "How Goop's Haters

Made Gwyneth Paltrow's Company Worth $250 Million" by Taffy Brodesser-Akner, *The New York Times Magazine*, July 25, 2018.

The Gwyneth Paltrow quote ("My life is good because . . .") is from the article "Paltrow Wastes No Time: Goop Is Thin" by Maria Russo, *Los Angeles Times*, September 26, 2008.

RAGE HOUSE
The Sia quote ("Um, mostly . . .") is from the article "How Sia Saved Herself" by Hillel Aron, *Rolling Stone*, September 2018.

THE GENIUS
The text message from Ben Rawluk to Jen Sookfong Lee appears courtesy of Ben Rawluk.

THE HOMELAND
The Bowen Yang quote ("This is the real crucible . . .") and the Awkwafina quote beginning "My whole life . . ." are from the article "You Know Awkwafina, But Have You Met Nora Lum?" by E. Alex Jung, *Harper's Bazaar*, February 2021.

The Awkwafina quote beginning "It's going to be hard . . ." is from the article "Awkwafina Never Thought She'd End Up Here" by Allison Glock, *Marie Claire*, September 2019.

THE PERFECT MOTHER
The quoted tweet by @jnajefferson was posted on September 22, 2017.

Kyrani Kanavaros

JEN SOOKFONG LEE was born and raised in Vancouver's East Side, and she now lives with her son in North Burnaby. Her books include *The Conjoined*, which was a finalist for the Ethel Wilson Fiction Prize and longlisted for the International DUBLIN Literary Award, *The Better Mother*, which was a finalist for the City of Vancouver Book Award, *The End of East*, *The Shadow List*, and *Finding Home*. Jen acquires and edits for ECW Press, and co-hosts the literary podcast *Can't Lit*.